Storyategy

Unlock the power of your brand
with a story based branding strategy

Hello

Welcome to "Storyategy" -
How to unlock the power of your brand
with a story based branding strategy

I'm Matt and I've got some
ideas to share.

STORYATEGY

HOW TO UNLOCK THE POWER OF YOUR BRAND WITH A STORY BASED BRANDING STRATEGY.

WRITTEN & PUBLISHED BY MATT DAVIES.

Copyright © 2018 Matt Davies

www.mrmattdavies.me

ISBN-13: 978-1717148629

ISBN-10: 171714862X

Edition 1.1

November 2018

Cover illustration by Lucy Goodwin

Instagram: @lostinlovebylucy, Etsy: lostinlovebylucy, Twitter: @lucyrosegoodwin

Portrait photograph on page 137 by Alex Bassford

Web: alexbassford.com Twitter: @alexbassford

This book is designed to help people like you. Business people who are driven towards a goal. Entrepreneurial people who want to make positive change and who are not satisfied with the status quo. The leaders. The thinkers. The drivers of their organisations.

I know your time is valuable so this book has been designed to be read in 5-6 hours. It can be read cover to cover but it has also been split into clear sections for easy reference.

The aim is to give you some powerful ideas with actionable exercises that can be used immediately.

The book is structured around a step by step process from which you will learn to set a brand strategy using a story. The process has 6 steps:

Although the process is universal, I know that every situation is unique. Therefore each of these steps has been split into three: Principles, Action and Outcome. Under the "Principles" section is an overview of the general concepts presented. Under "Action" suggested ways of discovering and then implementing your unique story are outlined. Under the "Outcome" section a clear list of the desired outcomes of the step is detailed. This structure has been used to make the ideas I am sharing not only interesting but practical to use.

Ready? Let's do this.

RO

IT ALL STARTS WITH PURPOSE

DO IT ON PURPOSE

What is leading the leaders?

Over the years I have seen the inside of many boardrooms and worked with marketing teams of all shapes and sizes. The most surprising thing I have discovered is that more often than not, what is holding a business back is, to put it bluntly, the people running the business themselves.

They don't deliberately do this of course; it's just that when it comes to teams of leaders - they all like to, well, lead. But what is leading the leaders? If there is no clear or serious top-level idea or strategy then everyone is pulling in their own direction. I'm not talking about details. I'm talking about a belief system which guides and informs decisions. Without this, communications become disjointed. Customers become confused as to what the brand stands for. Staff do not know how to behave. There is nothing to get behind and nothing to believe in.

Leaders gotta lead

The first step in the process is to define the meaning you want people to attach to the brand. Without the leaders knowing why they exist, how can anyone else in the business be expected to? The best way I have found to do this is the oldest and simplest way. To get the leaders in a room and facilitate constructive dialogue. Instead of allowing them to fight things out destructively these sessions need to ensure egos are left at the door. We will want ideas. Not egos.

In the foregoing chapters we will outline ways in which, when the leaders are gathered together, they can be guided through various activities and ways of thinking in order to unify them. Together they will be able to discover a compelling story and tell it. In this environment no ideas are worthless, however all ideas need to be given their proper place[1].

For these types of sessions, I also find it helpful to have people who are on the outer rings of the business in the room. People who deal with customers directly - like sales people. Sometimes it is also helpful to invite a customer into some of the sessions so that their perspective can be heard.

You will need to work in a timely, agile and flexible way. Every organisation and leader is different and therefore there is never a simple prescribed 'linear' process but rather landmarks on the road which need to be aimed for. That is why in this book I have simply outlined key milestones and provided tools to reach those, as opposed to being very prescribed and detailed. Sometimes items that have been decided upon early in the process need to be revisited - but that's okay. It's better to get it right than make poor decisions and rush it through.

Defining the meaning that people attach to your brand is only the beginning. You then need to find ways of ensuring you give this meaning the best possible chance of being discovered by your audience and look for ways to give them experiences which reinforce this meaning. Therefore later in the book we will also look at ideas of how to get the leadership on the same page in regards to this too.

The fact of the matter is that branding needs to start from *within* an organisation and be passionately driven by the leaders. It is way too important and almost impossible to simply be left to the marketing team. Apply branding to the inside before you apply it to the outside.

---

1 If you feel that this is going to be a huge challenge for your organisation, I'd suggest considering the principles of 'Parallel Thinking' as described by Edward de Bono in his book "Six Thinking Hats".

Purpose driven 'design thinking'

Whilst growing up I had a talent for hand drawing. I could make realistic sketches using nothing more than a pencil. One day, my father said to me that being an artist would only make money after I died - and so I dutifully looked around for a profession from which I could make a living. That's when I discovered and fell in love with 'design'. The difference between a graphic designer and an artist is the idea of 'purpose'. You do not simply use self-expression (like an artist does), your work serves a purpose. You work on behalf of a client to achieve their goal. You 'design' a solution to a problem. This purpose driven 'design thinking' has never left me and one of its outcomes is this book.

From very early on in my career as a graphic designer I found that design briefs often fell short of this very important aspect of design. To a designer 'purpose' should be everything - yet it is often missing.

I have become more and more aware that all leaders should be designers. Not necessarily in the conventional sense of putting pen to paper or pixel to screen but in the sense that leaders design solutions to problems. They create a vision in their minds of where they need to go and deliberately plan and execute on that plan, helping others along the way too. Therefore purpose is key. It motivates. It helps others join in. It connects people.

Briefs for design and marketing teams should be based on giving purpose led information to then allow design teams and marketing experts to respond in a meaningful way. Design should be driven by purpose not subjective artistic expression. Poor briefs are the main reason why projects of this type break down. *"They just don't get what we want"* the company says. *"They just don't know what they want"* the design team says. The thinking in this book has been born from such tensions.

Why don't briefs contain purpose?

But here is the killer question: Why don't briefs contain purpose? The truthful but painful answer is: Typically because the people writing the briefs do not know the real purpose themselves (or if we are being generous, they struggle to communicate a purpose).

How can an expert give advice to get you nearer to your goals if they are never told what those ultimate goals are? How can a team be effective without a direction? They need a mental end picture. A united one, which they can work towards. Not a picture made up of growth targets, key performance indicators and spreadsheets - but a more emotional picture of what a brand stands for, how it should communicate and how it should look. That is what this book is about. Over the years I have found ways of harmonising leadership teams in order for them to clarify their united purpose.

When this is done, these leadership teams can then effectively build brands that resonate authentically with their audiences and lead united teams. They can instinctively know if something is 'right'. They have a framework whereby they can test their ideas and behaviours. A framework based on purpose. A framework which is perpetually ingrained in a business or organisation so that it never looses sight of why it exists and whom it exists for.

I'm going to share a process and some powerful ideas with you to help you reach this goal.

So whether you are just starting a business, creating a new product or service or if you have been in the game for years and are trying to bring together the people around you, I hope you will find this book, and the ideas and tools shared, useful and powerful.

01

SKETCH THE PLOT & SET THE SCENE

PRINCIPLES

It has been well said that *"a journey of a thousand miles begins with a single step."*

As you start the process of thinking about your brand it's important to begin with the end in mind and sketch the basic framework upon which the detail will later be filled in.

It's also helpful at this early stage to define our terms and begin to unite our leaders around core principles.

You do not 'own' the 'brand'

In my experience, the average person believes that a logo is a 'brand'. From the outset let's be clear. Your logo is not your brand. This is far too small a definition. A well designed logo *alone* will not compel anyone to purchase a product or service - or even engage with it. A logo is part of a wider brand identity system which helps people to recognise a product or service. That is all. It is a sign post or a label.

I define brand as *the meaning* that people attach to your organisation, product or service. Other brilliant definitions I've come across are:

"what other people say about you when you're not in the room."[2]
Jeff Bezos, Technology Entrepreneur
& Founder of Amazon

"a person's gut feeling about a product, service or organization"[3]
Marty Neumeier, Writer & Director of Transformation at Liquid Agency

"the set of expectations, memories, stories and relationships that, taken together, account for a consumer's decision to choose one product or service over another."[4]
Seth Godin, Entrepreneur, Author & Speaker

"the total emotional experience someone has with you. "You" means all of your business's touch points - your website & social media presence, technology, team interactions, partnerships, loyalty programs, customer support, product purchases, product use."[5]
Jeffrey Davis M.A., Writer, Speaker, Consultant

---

2   Variously attributed. Source unknown.
3   *'The Brand Gap'*, AIGA Design Press, page 2, 2006
4   *'Define: Brand'*, Seth Godin blog, December 13 2009,
    sethgodin.typepad.com/seths_blog/2009/12/define-brand.html
5   *'The Motivation Behind Mission-Driven Brands'*, Psychology Today, January 2018
    www.psychologytoday.com/blog/tracking-wonder/201801/the-motivation-behind-mission-driven-brands

With this wider meaning we realise that brand is not something we simply dream up and tell other people about. Brand is what others say about us. It is an emotional meaning which exists in the hearts and minds of anyone who comes into contact with us. We do not control it. We do not own it. We can only influence it.

Businesses need to manage meaning

'Branding' is the attempt to *manage* that meaning. To seek to convey the right meaning to the right people.

Meaning is attached to a brand in many different ways by consumers. It could be how the brand presents itself, how it behaves, what it puts out on social media, how your people answer the phone or deal with complaints. It could be attached to what your product or service does or what it helps people achieve and feel.

Brand then, is the foundation of communications and business success - therefore, in my view, branding should also be the foundation of business strategy and behaviours. It touches everything and everyone.

Most organisations really struggle with this. Firstly there is a need to discover the authentic meaning of their brand. Their people not only need to understand this meaning but also believe in it so that it can be lived and expressed. Secondly they need to find a way of positioning and portraying the desired meaning to the outside world. All the time ensuring that as time goes on the work done does not get lost in the ether; and that as messaging cascades through the business there is always a simple way of checking whether activities are based on the core brand meaning.

There is also the key requirement for recruitment. A recent study on Millennials put it like this: *"Millennials recognize, absolutely, that financial success is one of the elements that characterize a "leading organization," but on its own is insufficient. Profit is combined with three other of the "Four Ps": people (employees and in wider society); products; and purpose, which, in combination, provide a platform for long-term success."[6]*

Therefore to attract and retain great employees, especially if they are young, knowing the purpose of your organisation and helping this be communicated and lived by your staff is very important.

These are crucial issues. Managing meaning is perhaps the most overlooked part of a business and yet it is perhaps the biggest factor which underpins growth. If you want to grow and thrive you need to manage meaning. You need to be a 'meaningful' business.

Stories give us meaning

The big question I have been asking for many years in the creative industries is: *What is the best way to create meaning?* The best answer I've come across: *Stories.*

Stories are the way we learn. They are how we make sense of everything around us. From when we are children reading fairy tales right up to modern documentaries and Hollywood blockbusters, stories help to ignite our imagination and compute the world that surrounds us and our part in it. What is our 'culture' if not a story told in a collective way?

We all see ourselves as the 'hero' of our own story. We call this 'self image' - an image we have of ourselves in our own minds. If, the reality of our lives fits with our self written story of ourselves and where we expect to be in life - then we are happy. If we feel we are behind or not living up to the story we have within our minds we feel unhappy. We write these subconscious stories ourselves.

As we live our lives we look around for other people to help us to get where we feel we should be in our story. We also do the same with brands.

6 *'Millennial Survey'*, Deloitte, 2016, www2.deloitte.com/content/dam/Deloitte/global/Documents/About-Deloitte/gx-millenial-survey-2016-exec-summary.pdf

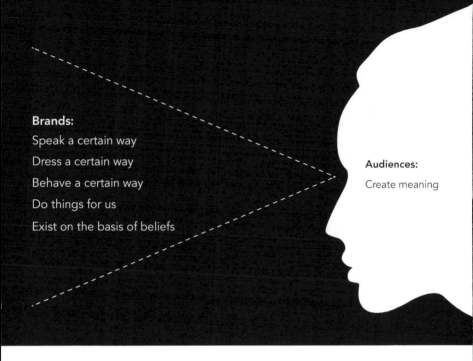

Brands:

Speak a certain way

Dress a certain way

Behave a certain way

Do things for us

Exist on the basis of beliefs

Audiences:

Create meaning

As with people, brands and the meaning we attach to them, help us to create meaning. They reinforce our belief systems. They help us explain who we are to others and ourselves. Psychology Today tells us that: *"consumers perceive the same type of personality characteristics in brands as they do in other people. And just like with people, they are attracted more to some personality types than others – attractions which are emotion based, not rational. Brand personality is communicated by marketers through packaging, visual imagery, and the types of words used to describe the brand."[7]*

Therefore consumers 'anthropomorphise' or personify brands. We think of them like we think of people, it's not hard to consider why. Think about it, brands:

- **Speak** - in the way they use text and sound.

- **Dress** - in how they use design and images to help us recognise them.

7   *'How Emotions Influence What We Buy'*, Peter Noel Murray Ph.D., Feb 26, 2013, www.psychologytoday. com/blog/inside-the- consumer-mind/201302/how-emotions-in uence-what-we-buy

- **Behave** - in who they connect with, events they hold, who they recruit and how those recruits interact with us.

- **Do** - they give out experiences, products and services which should improve our lives.

- **Believe** - they exist on the basis of a system of beliefs.

All of these things create meaning in our minds. Meaning which is closely related to how we have relationships with other humans.

Therefore as a consumer we look around for brands which stand for what we believe. We join brand belief systems if they are at harmony with our own. If they are not in line with our views we dislike them. If they cannot help us with our personal story of ourselves we are indifferent to them.

The key to branding is to ensure that we know why we exist and what we exist for. To tell an authentic story to attract a loyal brand audience to us and keep them winning. To convey meaning which supports the story our audience tells of themselves.

Going back in history, stories were used to teach lessons. They usually began by injecting fear into the hearer which resulted in the release of 'the fight or flight' hormone cortisol. When the fearful thing was then removed in the story the listeners brain released oxytocin, known as 'the love hormone', which makes you feel connected to your fellow humans. These things all generate emotion and 'meaning'.

Again in Psychology Today[8], the consumer psychology expert Peter Noel Murray, highlights the central role that emotion plays in consumer behaviour. In four points he shows the importance of marketing storytelling:

8 'How Emotions Influence What We Buy', Peter Noel Murray Ph.D., Feb 26, 2013, www.psychologytoday. com/blog/inside-the- consumer-mind/201302/how-emotions-in uence-what-we-buy

"When evaluating brands Functional MRI neuro-imagery shows that consumers primarily use emotions rather than information to make decisions. Advertising research has shown that consumers are more likely to buy a product because of the emotional response they feel to an advert, as opposed to the information and content of the advert's offer. According to research conducted by the Advertising Research Foundation, the emotion of "likeability" is the measure most predictive of whether an advertisement will increase a brand's sales. Studies show positive emotions toward a brand have far greater influence on consumer loyalty than trust and other judgments, which are based on a brand's attributes."

So, a person's feelings and experiences have far more influence on them making a purchase, than the facts or features on offer. Customers need to connect on an emotional level. Telling a story around 'why' you do what you do and not just presenting 'what' you do is therefore crucial.

The same article from Psychology Today goes on to state: *"the emotions that a brand evokes can be found in its "narrative" – the story that communicates "who" it is, what it means to the consumer, and why the consumer should care. This narrative is the basis for brand advertising and promotion. When everything is stripped back a brand, like a person, is simply a story. We are defined by the stories we tell... and that are told about us. And brands are part of that story".*

You therefore firstly need to discover your story, know who you are and what you stand for - and then tell that story through how you present each aspect of your business and customer experience. Steve Jobs, cofounder of Apple Inc, was reported to have once said *"the most powerful person in the world is the story teller..."*[9]

9   Quora comment by Tomas Higbey 'What are the best stories about people randomly (or non-randomly) meeting Steve Jobs?', 2013, www.quora.com/Steve-Jobs/What-are-the-best-stories-about-people-randomly-or-non-randomly-meeting-Steve-Jobs/answer/Tomas-Higbey?share=1&srid=eLr

Stories add value

Can it really be that simple? Is everything just a story?

If you are still sceptical about this story telling approach, consider the fact that you can get a product, made in the same factory, with the same ingredients and the same packaging and slap two labels on it. Because of what is printed on the labels, some customers will be willing to pay more for one of the labelled products than the other. Why? Because one label tells a story which aligns with a customer's belief system and how they see themselves and they will be willing to pay extra for this. This is how branding works. It helps to communicate value and meaning.

We all have stuff, what we want is meaning.

If you know your brand's story, if you understand your audience and the meaning they want, then you can have a framework on which to handle all of your communications. You will have a purposeful meaning in the way you portray your brand creatively, in the way your business needs to behave, innovate, recruit, deal with customers, allow customers to experience its products and many other things.

200%
increase in
perceived value

Same product. Different story.

Source:
Tesco.com.
Prices as of
April 2018.

£0.25
Tesco Everyday Value Baked Beans

£0.75
Heinz Baked Beanz

A brand story has huge benefits

I passionately believe that when a leadership
team is united around a common brand
story it has the following benefits:

- **Unification**
  It unifies the leadership team and therefore
  saves time as there is less conflict.

- **Attraction**
  It gets people onside. It will attract passionate
  customers and new recruits who believe the same
  as you and who stand for the same things.

- **Addition of value**
  When it has been executed and gains traction,
  customers will be prepared to pay more for
  the value of the meaning the brand offers.

- **Clearer communications**
  It informs marketing and advertising initiatives
  and gives a framework for making decisions.

- **Minimisation of subjectivity**
  It generates the basis of a clear, purpose
  driven, creative brief around how the brand
  should be positioned and visually portrayed.

- **Differentiation**
  It helps businesses stand out in their marketplace.

- **Clearer business strategy**
  It helps to give form to the behaviours
  of the business and inform the types of
  new products or services the brand might
  develop and offer in the future.

A brand story explains why

A brand story is actually a summary of the emotional story you would like to be in the mind of your audience. It should explain what you stand for (and by implication, what you don't). It should contain aspiration and belief in something which will never be compromised. It will contain ideas which your audience can get behind. It will focus on why you exist and it needs defining so it can be told and lived.

I often come across 'our story' sections on business to business websites which go something like this:

> "The company was started in 1992 by our founder Larry Smith in Leeds... The company went on to win the Yorkshire maintenance company of the year award in 1999 and grew to 32 staff... In 2005 the company acquired ABC Ltd and added a logistics division. This enabled the company to deliver goods faster... In 2016 the company reached a significant milestone and turned over £5 million with 103 staff covering the whole of the UK. In 2018 Larry Smith retired and his son, Barry Smith, has now taken over..."

My question to 'stories' like this is: who cares? This is a story that focuses on *what* not why. 'Why' is where we can connect emotionally. The 'what' is not emotional. There is nothing here to get behind, nothing to join, nothing to believe in. The above story shows all of the hallmarks of a business focused on making money and that does not appreciate or understand the value of their products and services in the mind of the customer.

A brand story should put the customer at the heart of why the company exists.

An example of a short empathetic and emotional brand story for this example would be:

> "Like you, we passionately believe that every second counts and we know that in the engineering industry time is everything. When a machine is down, every second is costing money. We exist to eliminate non-productivity from our client's manufacturing lines due to machine breakdown. We imagine a world where no down time exists. We bring control and order to the potential chaos of breakdown. Regular servicing of machines, preemptive replacements and speedy delivery of parts is how we have made a name for ourselves. ABC Ltd. Time is everything."

In this crude example you can see how there is emotion, empathy and something to believe in. If I owned a production line I would be interested in speaking to this maintenance company - not simply because of what they do but because of why they do it. Instead of speaking at the audience and dictating that ABC Ltd. will make a difference, this story gets the audience on side and shares a vision of the future.

As a talented engineer looking for a job I would imagine this type of company would be innovative and value improvements because of why they do what they do. I'd be keen to join it because I could add value if I also believed in these things.

Staff of ABC Ltd would have a clear way of recognising if they were indeed 'living the brand' with their actions or if they were falling short.

Stories bring people together.

A brand vision brings focus

In the Bible there is a wise proverb which states:

"Where there is no vision, the people perish"[10]

The idea of this proverb is that with no vision of where you are going, what to believe in and a mental picture of how to get there, the people will lose their way. How true this is.

In his international best selling self improvement book *"Seven Habits of Highly Effective People"*, Stephen. R. Covey's second habit is *"Begin with the end in mind"*. He explains:

"Begin with the end in mind is based on the principle that all things are created twice. There's a mental or first creation, and a physical or second creation to all things"[11]

In other words one has to imagine the solution to a problem. There has to be an imaginary 'vision' of the world a brand is seeking to achieve. This is created mentally before people can join this idea and help make it become a reality.

Business coach, Simon Sinek, has a popular TED Talk and has written a book on this subject called *"Start with Why"*[12]. In his book he states:

"People don't buy what you do, they buy WHY you do it"[13]

He explains that communicating WHY we do things is what emotionally connects us with others who believe what we believe.

Clarifying your "why" in a concise and clear vision statement can therefore be extremely powerful.

---

10 Proverbs 29:18, The Bible.
11 *'Seven Habits of Highly Effective People'* by Stephen. R. Covey, page 99
12 For further information about how to find your why see also *'Find your Why'*, Portfolio Penguin, by David Mead and Peter Docker.
13 *'Start with Why'*, Portfolio Penguin, by Simon Sinek, Page 41.

There are typically three types of vision statement - ones that focus on:

- **Belief** - an ideology for which the brand stands for

- **Passion** - something the brand and its followers are passionate about

- **Cause** - a problem or obstacle which needs to be overcome

In his book *"Traction"*, Gino Wickman has a whole segment of his 'Entrepreneurial Operating System' (EOS) dedicated to *"Vision"*. He suggests that the following eight points should be checked off:

1. It's stated in three to seven words

2. It's written in simple language

3. It's big and bold

4. It has an 'aha' effect

5. It comes from the heart

6. It involved everyone

7. It's not about money

8. It's bigger than a goal

However you do it, it is crucial to have a brand 'vision' which is defined and understood by your team. These eternal principles of vision and purpose are a crucial foundational element to branding. To manage the meaning people attach to a brand it must know why it exists. It must have a vision for the world it operates in and it must be able to articulate this if it wants customers and staff to become loyal to it and become passionate for it.

Vision brings a focus on meaning and purpose. Let's focus.

Can your customers
and your people see
your brand clearly?

ACTIONS

It is important how this initial workshop session is introduced to the leadership group. Explain that no idea is a bad idea. Explain the desired outcomes.

It would be very much worth reviewing or presenting a few of the principles we have outlined in this section to the group. This will help them understand the importance of the task ahead of them.

Once they have grasped the principles, it will be time to set the task of laying some key foundations to what will follow later in the Storyategy process, through a variety of exercises. In this section I have given suggested workshop tasks which I have found to be very effective - even amongst leadership teams which are very factious.

As each session continues, decisions are layered on top of decisions, meaning we will take everyone on the journey with us.

Sketch the plot

Purpose
This exercise helps to relax the participants and immediately get them stuck into something positive. We want them to begin to think about their purpose, the reason for the brand's existence and its future - this exercise helps the group to do this.

Method
Get the group to write a 'beginning','middle' and 'end' for the brand. Explain that this is just a starting point for the brand - not the final story and the things outlined may change as we go through the process.

The 'beginning' of the plot should be focused on how the brand began, the big idea behind its birth and the challenges that were overcome to launch it. The 'middle' should be about what's happening now - what are the main issues affecting the brand? The 'end' is the big one because this is where the group will need 'vision' to look forward. They should imagine the world in 50 years time. What has the brand achieved? What was it known for? How did the brand die and what killed it?

Depending on the amount of leaders in a workshop I would usually set this task for them to do in pairs or small groups. This encourages interaction. After an allotted time, gather the group around and white board each group's ideas. Where different or even opposing ideas are shared, get them on the white board and allow for discussion to take place around the conflict areas (but keep things positive!).

Fill in 'The Brand Triangle'

Purpose

In this section of the workshop we will be tentatively completing 'The Brand Triangle' diagram shown on the right. This triangle really gets to the core of a brand and in one diagram helps to explain the guiding principles of the brand's purpose. At this stage we will again ask the leaders to put down their initial gut feelings as these may change as time goes on.

Method

Ask the group to individually write down 'why' the brand exists. If the group struggles, ask them to write a vision statement for the brand or to explain the purpose of the brand[14]. A good question to ask might be: *"if there were no barriers, what is it this brand will strive to accomplish?"* If this is still too difficult, get the group to consider what they passionately believe in. Get the group to do this based on the rough plot from the previous exercise. This is where they can really 'think big'. The 'why' should be something almost unattainable but which drives the brand forward to continue to innovate towards it. Discuss the responses as a group and, if possible, create a 'why' statement that everyone can agree to.

A why statement might begin with the following examples:

"We believe that..."

"Our purpose is to..."

"We envisage a world where..."

Fill in the 'why' segment of The Brand Triangle.

For the 'who' segment we will be looking at workshop exercises to really 'design' an audience later in

---

14 See page 22.

The Brand Triangle

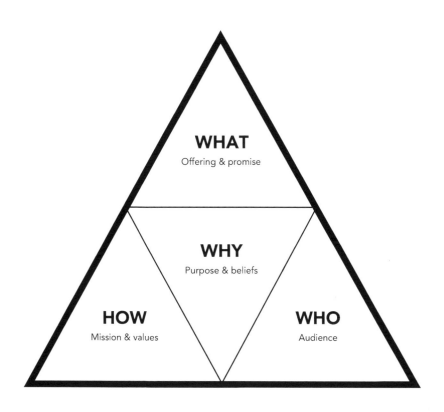

WHAT
Offering & promise

WHY
Purpose & beliefs

HOW
Mission & values

WHO
Audience

the process. At this early stage it is good to get a rough feel for who the leaders think their audience is. Something quite over arching is okay for this stage. Get the group to summarise who they think the brand serves, get them to discuss and agree a top line definition and fill in the 'who section'.

Now do the same for the 'How' section. This, in effect, is the mission of the brand. It usually starts with "By... ". Depending on the needs of the group you can eventually revisit this and really get into some detail around long term and short term goals. For an initial brand exercise I would suggest keeping this quite light in terms of detail. List out the values (key beliefs or behaviours) the leaders desire their staff to embody as they complete the 'why' of the brand.

As you come to the 'What' section you can get quite detailed here if you need to. Some groups like to map out all of their products and product categories. Some like to map out their brand architecture and the different businesses in their group. There is huge value in mapping out all of the functions of a business[15]. For a brand workshop though, I'd suggest this is done at a later time and that you keep the 'what' quite general. I find one way of doing this well is to ask the leaders if the brand was going to promise something, what would it be?

Now you have completed the brand triangle, get this initial version typed up and hung somewhere prominent, so it can be seen in all future brand workshop sessions. Having this placed somewhere visible as you go through a process like this, can help you to see areas which are currently outside of the authenticity of the brand and hence why certain problems exist. Ensure this version is called a draft - as it might be worth revisiting as the process goes on.

---

15 See 'Traction - Get a Grip on Your Business', 2012, Gino Whitman
   as a good example of how to do this in-depth.

OUTCOMES

Results

As a group you will have:

- **Sketched your plot**
  Roughly sketched a beginning, middle and end plot line for the brand

- **Drafted your 'Brand Triangle'**
  Defined the brand's 'Why', 'Who', 'How' and 'What'

Through the process

At the end of this first step "Sketch the plot and set the scene" your aim is to have facilitated the leaders to agree the brand's purpose and reason to exist. You will have begun to unite them around the start of a strategy and vision, in a nonthreatening, interesting and fun way, which is outside the typical, dull 'business-speak' they might be used to.

The things defined may, and probably will, need revisiting in the future but that's okay and hopefully they will be motivated to passionately continue with the process.

02

DESIGN YOUR AUDIENCE

PRINCIPLES

Without a focus on who your audience is, the modern business will fail. Any sales, marketing or branding activity is ultimately destined to become useless if it is not directed towards those to whom it desires to serve.

In today's world the customer is everything. They have the power. They control success. Customers create brands and they own them.

The aim of the game is to set things up so that they can get behind your brand and carry it forward.

If they win. You win.

Brands must be customer centric

It used to be the case that businesses would invent a product, then go out and look for customers to buy it. This was 'business centric' but this way of things is changing. In this post-modern world we are not looking for more stuff. We are seeking meaning. As time goes on, customers are becoming less interested in the 'what' because they could get the same type of product from any number of stores or websites. What they are becoming more and more interested in is the 'why'. Meaning is everything in market places which have become saturated - and it is in this that consumers place value.

Therefore if we are going to build a truly successful brand which has longevity in the hearts and minds of the customer, we need to shift focus from *what* we are producing. Instead we need to turn our attention to why it's helpful to the people it is designed for and why we are inventing and bringing products to market. We then need to look for the next helpful thing we could produce for the same audience, so that they keep winning. This is how great brands are built. Brands are movements which have an appeal to audiences when they promise something of worth to them.

This means you have to start with the customer. You then invent products or services (or both) for the customer, which in turn creates a brand that sustains your business. Constant innovation is key to upholding your brand's promise.

As an example of this you might consider the Harley Davidson motorcycle brand[16]. This brand knows its customers inside and out. It understands their motivation to rebel from the norm and get out and explore the open roads at the weekends. It is this need it appeals to. It designs its products and whole customer experience around fulfilling these customer

---

16 www.harley-davidson.com

desires. When a customer buys a Harley Davidson it says something about the customer. Just owning a Harley Davidson has meaning. It means you believe in freedom and in breaking out of everyday normality to explore new places. If a customer wanted to add further meaning and express themselves even more then they could seek to join the "Hells Angels" in their local area and go for communal rides and meet ups with other people who believe what they believe. They could align themselves with other Harley fans and connect to a shared identity. This could all become so powerful that a customer might even consider tattooing the Harley Davidson brand identity into their flesh permanently. Not because Harley Davidson sells a machine but because Harley Davidson means so much to the consumer. Because the brand represents an attitude.

You see, it's not about the business. It's about the customer. Aligning the brand with their beliefs, desires and needs. Being customer centric is the key to building a brilliant brand which is passionately followed and loved. Solving the customer's problems and adding meaning to the lives of the customer is the key.

Who is the brand's audience? What is the goal or challenge of that audience? What is their personal story and how do we, as a character in their story, add value and help them achieve that goal or overcome that challenge? In the case of Harley Davidson, the customer is a 'rebel-explorer' character seeking to break free. The Harley Davidson brand and customer experience masterfully mirrors this by becoming the vehicle[17] for this expression. It does this in the way it communicates, how it behaves, the products it invents and ultimately the meaning it injects into the customer's life - which is why it is so successful.

---

17 Please excuse the pun.

The way customers think about brands has changed

Over time, the value we attach to products and services has changed[18]. This is partly due to the increase in availability of similar products through new capabilities in communication and technology.

Around 100 years ago in the industrial era, the 'market places' of the world were uncluttered. The way products were marketed was on the basis of what a product was and what features it had. When consumers became used to being told what a product was, and other, more refined products came to market with the same features, the focus shifted to product benefits. The slight advantages of a product became the key driver of the advertising in order to get noticed. The more things that the product had, the better the product. As time went on and competing products developed similar refined features, market places once again became saturated. Due to this, marketing shifted to focus on the experience of the product in order to differentiate offerings. How the product made a customer feel as they used it and engaged with the business that sold it. All of these things were based on marketers attempting to find ways to interrupt a consumer's life to tell them about their product - but now, with the technology available to us things are very different.

A consumer is now only two voice commands away from being able to obtain a product at any moment of the day. In this sense, the resources available to us are higher now than ever before in the history of the world. However, when that consumer hits their smart phone, there are so many products that do exactly the same thing it is difficult for them to make a decision as to which product they should choose. From a marketing perspective the biggest challenge therefore is to stand out in the crowded marketplace.

18 For more information on this see 'The evolution of marketing' in
   'The Brand Gap', page 39, by Marty Neumeier.

How do brands stand out today? By putting the customer first.

Although the features, benefits and experience of the product are all still important, what has become the new best thing to focus on is what the product says about the customer. The brands which succeed in saturated market places are the ones which stand for something because they help customers self identify. They help customers reinforce the story they have created about themselves in their own mind[19]. They help customers express themselves and explain to the world who they are.

Referencing a study being conducted by BeyondThePurchase.Org, Ryan T. Howell, an Assistant Professor of Psychology at San Francisco State University states:

"By definition, materialists place a greater emphasis on tangible items as indicators of identity and success, often believing that acquiring goods leads to happiness. More specifically, materialists buy products that signal their identity (such as clothes)... Thus, they are more likely to respond emotionally to the items and marketing messages they encounter."[20]

All of these things: features, benefits, experience and identification are now important to the modern consumer of a brand. You need to know and understand all of these to effectively position a brand. However the hardest and most powerful is the final aspect: self identification. This is what makes you stand out from the crowd. Ask yourself, what does it mean to a consumer to buy my product or service? What does it say about that person? This is the key to unlocking the power of meaning and once you understand this you

---

19 In his book '*The Culting of Brands*', researcher Douglas Atkin goes to great lengths to explain the connection between members of cults and the extreme followers of brands. He shows that the religious systems which help to give people purpose, meaning and beliefs are traits which brands that attract 'cult-like' followings also embody.
20 '*What Motivates People to Buy Compulsively?*', Psychology Today, August 2012, www.psychologytoday.com/blog/cant-buy-happiness/201208/what-motivates-people-buy-compulsively.

can then design the whole experience of a customer to enhance this meaning and the consumer's identity.

To do this effectively a brand has to stand for a set of beliefs and live by them - thus attracting an audience who also believe what the brand believes[21].

The way customers buy has changed

The way we buy has radically changed in the last 20 years. 20 years ago the knowledge (and therefore power) was all in the hands of the seller. They knew the price of what they were selling compared to the competition. They knew the other alternatives on the market. They knew how the product was made, what was likely to make it break and why their product was better. Or not. With the spread of readily available information via the internet, that has all changed. Not only can we do independent research around a product, its price and its competition, we can now go much deeper into why the company that makes it exists at all. We can see if their story fits with ours. We can also read what other people think about that product or service and we can check how authentic this brand really is.

Now the power is in the hands of the consumer - not the seller.

All of this has only been possible because of advances in technology and the impact the internet has made into the consciousness of our lives. Not only has the knowledge available to us increased, but technology has also given us the ability to screen out unwanted adverts and interruptions. For these reasons the old techniques of advertising which were born in the pre-internet era have ceased to be as effective as they were previously.

---

21 As evidence of this in the 2017 Edelman Earned Brand report of the 14,000 respondents from 14 countries, 50% identified themselves as "belief-driven". 67% of these claimed to have made a first time purchasing decision because they agreed with a brand's position on a topic. 65% stated they would not buy from a brand when it stays silent on an issue they feel it has an obligation to address. Other reports could be sighted which inform us that this 'belief-driven' purchasing trend is increasing.

The way the old model worked was simple.

When advertising a product, interrupt someone's day through a magazine advert, TV commercial, cold call etc., tell them about the product and then they have a choice - buy it or not.

Most people did not buy, but in a mass market the small percentage that did gave you revenue. If you made a profit from this you simply reinvested in more advertising and out came more profit. Bingo.

The problem here though is that this is no longer working in the information rich, interruption-weary modern consumer.

They will not buy your product simply because you have interrupted their day and shown it to them. They want to buy on their terms. If they have a problem they will go off and research it - in their own time. You now have to compete like never before but not through interrupting people, rather by letting them come to you. You have to be authentic, else when the consumer peruses your brand online and comes across poor reviews they will doubt you. You are now one of hundreds if not thousands of products or services in a global marketplace. How do you stand out? It all comes down to effective branding and communicating the meaning of why you exist and who you exist for. It comes down to how best you are helping the customer with their goals and challenges and how accessible that help is to them. It comes down to providing content and experiences that help the customer so that they believe you and buy from you.

It's not about *you*. It's about *them*.

Now the physical quality of your product has to be matched by an emotional quality for the customer - and that comes from good branding, from managing meaning.

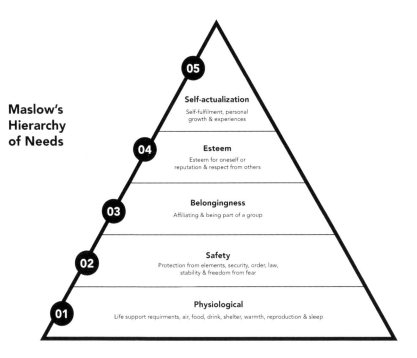

Maslow's Hierarchy of Needs

05

Self-actualization
Self-fulfilment, personal growth & experiences

04

Esteem
Esteem for oneself or reputation & respect from others

03

Belongingness
Affiliating & being part of a group

02

Safety
Protection from elements, security, order, law, stability & freedom from fear

01

Physiological
Life support requirments, air, food, drink, shelter, warmth, reproduction & sleep

The customer motivations

In consumer behaviour theories there are some interesting models which are worth considering when shining the spotlight on your brand's audience.

A model which can be most helpful is "Maslow's Hierarchy of Needs"[22] which outlines categories of human need in five priorities.

Maslow taught that people are motivated to achieve specific needs and that certain needs take precedence over others. In his model, the most basic need is for physical survival. If this is not satisfied then this will be the first thing that motivates our behaviour. Once this level of need is fulfilled, the next level up is what motivates us and so on. The ultimate need is "self actualization".

Knowing which band your audience is operating at is extremely helpful and we will layer meaning on top of this in upcoming chapters. For now please review Maslow's law above.

22 Abraham Maslow, 'A Theory of Human Motivation', 1943.

ACTIONS

Getting a leadership team to acknowledge and think deeply about the audience they serve, is one of the key stepping stones in steering a brand into being customer centric. Doing this helps the leadership team begin to make decisions based on who the brand exists for - not on their own personal opinions and ambitions.

But beware. These activities do mean the group will need to be brave, for if you are looking to help a specific audience you will be excluding others.

Depending on the size of your organisation and depth of knowledge within it, this step in the process can become quite a challenge. Lack of insights into who the current audience of the brand is, or a plethora of products and services designed for a wide array of audiences, can make things tricky. If either of these is the case in your organisation, I would suggest these issues are highlighted to the leadership team as areas to get better clarity on. However, they should not hold up the process. This stage lets you design and define the audience for your brand which may not exist at this moment in time.

Define your audience categories

Purpose

This is the first step in defining who
the brand should be serving.

The idea here is to see how, in the minds
of the leadership team, their current
audience groups are categorised.

It allows you to uncover potential issues in
relation to knowledge gaps, or too wide
a brand audience, very early on.

Method

Split into groups. Define internal and external
audiences. At this stage it's about rough categories
of audiences. Start for example with very high
levels of category: "suppliers", "customers",
"staff". Then get each workshop group to identify
further sub categories of the types of audiences.

After a set time, gather the workshop groups
together and discuss the results of each group.

Refine the categories and see if a
consensus can be made.

Define your audience personas

Purpose

Personas help to "humanise" decisions and to really think about the types of people your brand is designed to appeal to.

In this section of a workshop, you want to obtain a good idea of the types of audiences sitting within the audience categories that the group has agreed on.

Method

An audience persona is a semi-fictional character which represents a type of audience. You can get really deep into what your organisation knows about these generalised types of audiences but I always think the following model is a helpful start. I call it the '6 Persona Ps':

- **Past** - what have they been doing up until this point? How have they got into this life situation or job role? Why did they begin in the profession or set out on the path?

- **Present** - what are they doing right now?

- **Pain** - what are their challenges? What friction is in their lives?

- **Passions** - what do they believe in? What makes them tick and get excited?

- **Problems we can solve** - what problems does our product or service solve for this persona?

- **Performance judgment** - how will they judge our brand's performance?

Make these audiences memorable. I have found a really good way of doing this is to use alliteration between a word representing a person's job or type, and then a name. For example "Corporate Clive" or "Maintenance Mike" are great names for personas as they ensure everyone can begin to use a common language around audience types. Another mechanism which helps, is to get illustrations to represent them.

Once the group has set out these personas they need to be refined and reviewed. Take a step back and look at the results. The leadership team should be asked who the primary audiences are and why. Who should the brand focus on? Ideally there would only be one or two primary audiences because this allows real focus. If the brand has a wide amount of audiences, this should be acknowledged as a huge challenge and rather than one brand, a set of multiple brands need to be considered to focus on specific audiences. Remember, this is about making things easier for customers, not making them easier for the business.

One key thing that needs to be acknowledged in this exercise is that in order to stand for something you cannot be all things to all people. Design your audience based around the 'Brand Triangle' from the first step. Who is the brand *really* aligned to? Are some personas there because they make the brand money but are not actually a key audience for the brand to fulfil it's why? Which personas believe what the brand believes? Who does the brand like doing business with best? Who are the easiest audiences for the brand to get along with?

If further market research needs to be conducted to back up any assumptions the group has made, then this should be commissioned at this stage to verify the personas created.

As a side point, it can be helpful to review your business' Customer Relationship Software and website to see if data can be segmented into these persona types. You can then consider what tracking, reporting, and feedback systems you have in place to help you better serve the target personas. If the business can communicate with a specific set of personas then this can become a powerful tool to help add insight into future activities. The personas can also become a key sales and marketing tool; for example, as the basis of a website or marketing campaign brief.

Define your key customer need

Purpose

To help the leadership team understand the basic human needs that their brand is serving.

Method

Review Maslow's Hierarchy of needs. For each persona, define the category of need the audience sits within.

Once all personas have a level, consider which level is most prevalent. This will become the 'key customer need' which you will need to begin to focus on.

Write the 'key customer need' somewhere that can be clearly seen in the upcoming sessions.

Once you are happy with your audience personas it is a good idea that they are taken away and typed up as 'persona cards' - which can be given out or pinned up to remind the group of the audiences they are seeking to serve.

OUTCOMES

Results

As a group you will have completed:

- **Audience categories**
  The general categories of audience that your
  brand will be looking to engage with.

- **Audience personas**
  Personas for each of the audience types
  which sit within each category. Persona cards
  representing each of these. A clear understanding
  of customer needs aligned with Maslow's law.

Through the process

You will have, as a group, made decisions
on who you are seeking to attract and
appeal to, as well as who you are not.

The exercise should have focused the leadership's
minds on the brand audience in a relatable way.
The audience personas (the "Who" of the Brand
Triangle) will have been designed in line with the other
parts of the Brand Triangle and will form the focal
point of what follows in the Storyategy process.

03

DISCOVER YOUR ARCHETYPAL CHARACTERS

PRINCIPLES

At this stage of the process I now want to introduce you to some powerful tools that I have found to be very effective in unifying a team and in setting a brand strategy.

In this step we are going to 'piggy back' on existing mental frameworks which are inherent in mankind. We are going to draw on some basic ideas from psychology and use them to our advantage.

This will help us communicate in a stronger and clearer way to our target audience and help our messaging have deeper emotional meaning.

We anthropomorphise brands

As we have already mentioned in step 1[23], humans tend to "anthropomorphise" or "personify" brands. That is, the way we make sense of them is to think of them as other humans.

This is very interesting because it means that how and what brands communicate, will directly affect purchasing decisions. The perceived meaning around this brand "personality" that forms in our audience's minds will either attract or repel them. If we are to manage this meaning, then it is essential we get to grips with our brand personality. This will enable us to ensure it is authentic - so that the right meaning about our brand is understood by the right people.

But how do we uncover the right personality? Also, and perhaps more importantly, how do we ensure we are authentic? The best method I have found to help us with this is 'archetypal branding'.

The Swiss psychiatrist Carl Jung founded analytical psychology. Around 1919, he defined the idea of 'archetypes' as patterns of behaviour that reflect typical human characters. Although defined by Jung, the origins of "archetypes" goes back to the classical era and perhaps beyond, into the prehistorical mist of time.

The root words that make up the English word "archetype" are Greek. They are "archein", which means "original or old"; and "typos", which means "pattern, model or type". When combined, these words mean an "original pattern" from which all other similar ideas are derived or emulated.

Carl Jung
1875 - 1961

23 See 'Stories give us meaning' page 14.

Jung described archetypes as: *"Forms or images of a collective nature which occur practically all over the earth as constituents of myths and at the same time as autochthonous[24], individual products of the unconscious origin"*[25]. Jung explains that we have something called the *"collective unconscious"* - this is a way of thinking which connects all of us as humans, across time and across culture. He says *"The archetype is a tendency to form such representations of a motif - representations that can vary a great deal in detail without losing their basic pattern... They are, indeed, an instinctive trend, as marked as the impulse of birds to build nests, or ants to form organised colonies"*[26]. Within this, archetypes play a role as we recognise them unconsciously and then our conscious minds add meaning to them.

Jung's theories were far reaching, helping to define human psychology itself and influencing well known psychologists such as Freud.

Jon Howard-Spink, an advertising strategist, has defined an archetype as; *"a universally familiar character or situation that transcends time, place, culture, genre and age. It represents an eternal truth"*[27].

Out of Jung's work, twelve character archetypes have been identified which people embody at different times in their life and which are the basis of their personality construct . These are evoked depending on the type of person, what that person desires to do or the situation the person finds themselves in. These 'archetypal characters' are amplified in stories, which is why they are extremely useful to the branding process because they are part of our 'mental architecture'. Consequentially, they evoke deep-seated emotions in us. They convey unexplained meaning which audiences instinctively appreciate.

---

24 *"Autochthonous - of an inhabitant of a place, indigenous rather than descended from migrants or colonists."* Oxford Dictionary.
25 *'Psychology and Religion'*, Carl Jung, 1958.
26 *'Approaching The Unconscious'*, *'Man and his symbols'*, Carl Jung, 1964.
27 *'Using archetypes to build stronger brands'*, Admap, Oct 2002.

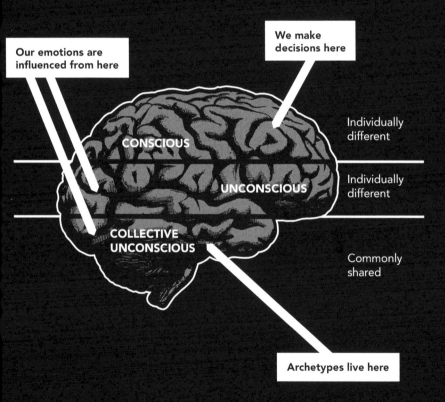

Our emotions are
influenced from here

We make
decisions here

CONSCIOUS

UNCONSCIOUS

COLLECTIVE
UNCONSCIOUS

Individually
different

Individually
different

Commonly
shared

Archetypes live here

We all enjoy stories which have powerful, relatable characters. It is most likely that these characters embody archetypes. It doesn't matter if we are reading an ancient Greek myth, listening to an Aboriginal tribal story or watching a modern Hollywood movie, we will come across the same types of characters. We know them. We understand them. They are universal, transcending culture and demographics.

To realise the power of archetypes one has only got to think about the popularity and success of films such as Star Wars, Lord of the Rings, Harry Potter, the DC Super Heroes and other stories featuring iconic heros.

Archetypes represent the fears, drivers, needs, and desires of us all and are hard-wired into everyone. When we desire to achieve a particular goal, these archetypes are triggered and we embody them or seek them to help us on our mission. They are *amplified* in stories.

Archetypes provide a framework for managing the meaning of your brand

When it comes to branding, archetypes are one of the most powerful tools I have found to help get leadership teams on the same page, and to create a meaningful basis for positioning brands.

In their book entitled "The Hero and the Outlaw"[28], authors Margaret Mark and Carol S. Pearson demonstrate how Jungian archetypes have enabled companies to powerfully manage the meaning of branded products and services. Top brands which embody archetypes, either deliberately or accidently, get the most traction and generate emotion and passion within their internal teams and external

---

28 *'The Hero and the Outlaw: Building Extraordinary Brands Through the Power of Archetypes'*, McGraw-Hill, Margaret Mark & Carol S. Pearson, 2001.
Note: Many of the things in the following section of this book are based on this work. If you wish to have a deep understanding of the way this works I recommend reading it. I am not seeking to obtain any credit for this fantastic masterpiece of insight into branding but only wish to highlight it as a helpful tool within the Storyategy system.

customers. Mark and Pearson show how these archetypes connect with a number of scientifically defined audience motivations. By understanding which archetype helps to tell the right story to the right audience, a system can be developed which helps to identify which brand archetype a business might be. This framework can then be used to ensure all communications are consistent and clear, projecting authentic meaning to an audience.

In today's highly competitive market places, communicating your purpose to your target audience well, is one of the keys to developing a successful business swiftly. Archetypes provide a way to do this and enable a brand to stand out from the crowd. They represent the brand's purpose in a form that audiences can quickly and easily recognise and form the bedrock of the creative look and feel, tone of voice and behaviours of a brand's activities. Ultimately they enable you to tell a better story which resonates deeply within an audience.

I have found that they also help to unify a leadership team. This could be because they provide a 'non threatening' and fun way to think about business which is authentic. Because the archetypes are familiar and positive, this also adds to the experience and can help energise teams to fall in love again with what they do.

Archetypal branding is a fundamental tool in the branding toolkit and an ingenious way for the management of meaning which is aligned with customer motivations.

The way Mark & Pearson's system works is based on multiple motivational theories. They explain that depending on what a customer is desiring, this motivation can be mapped to Jungian archetypes and can be used as a framework for adding brand personality.

Brand archetype map

Based on the model by Margaret Mark & Carol S. Pearson
in their book "The Hero & The Outlaw"

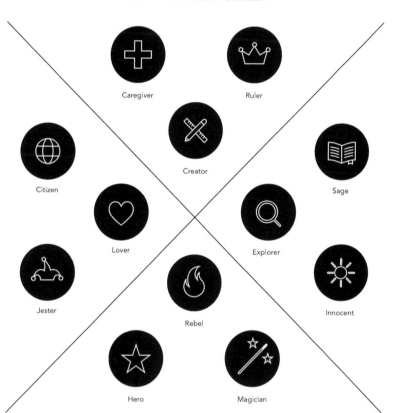

Customer motivation: **SAFETY & STABILITY**

Caregiver

Ruler

Creator

Citizen

Sage

Lover

Explorer

Jester

Innocent

Rebel

Hero

Magician

Customer motivation: **BELONGING & RELATIONSHIPS**

Customer motivation: **INDEPENDENCE & SELF-ACTUALISATION**

Customer motivation: **MASTERY & ESTEEM**

There are four motivations which come in opposite pairs[29]. For example, we are motivated to belong to a wider group or community and connect in relationships; this is offset by our human desire to be independent. The two motivations pull us in different directions. Likewise we seek to be safe; this is offset against the need for excitement and to obtain mastery over risk.

These motivations align with Abraham Maslow's 'Hierarchy of Needs' which we have previously reviewed.[30]

We have summarised each motivation as follows:

- **Safety & Stability**
  (Maslow's Hierarchy of Needs Level 2)

- **Belonging & Relationships**
  (Maslow's Hierarchy of Needs Level 3)

- **Mastery & Esteem**
  (Maslow's Hierarchy of Needs Level 4)

- **Independence & Self-actualisation**
  (Maslow's Hierarchy of Needs Level 5)

The summary model shown on the facing page presents these customer motivations as four quadrants. 'Belonging' on the left and 'Independence' on the right. 'Stability' on the top and 'Mastery' on the bottom. The archetypes which are evoked by each motivation are then mapped accordingly.

Use this framework to help you identify which archetype your brand might be.

29 See 'The Hero and the Outlaw' pages 14-18, 'A System That Integrates Motivational and Archetypal Theory' for more in-depth information about this framework
30 See page 39 'The customer motivations'.

The twelve brand archetypes

In the following pages I have set out a brief summary of the twelve archetypes[31] based on Mark and Pearson's model. I have also given an example of various brands which are embodying each of these archetypes. Each of these twelve archetypes align to one of the four paired customer motivations. These become the basis for creating powerful brand stories and managing the meaning of a brand.

01. The Innocent

The Innocent is all about wanting to experience paradise and their motives are almost childlike. They simply want to be happy. They do not want to tread on anyone's toes to obtain their dreams. They value doing things right and hate to disappoint. They see the world through rose-tinted spectacles and everything is just lovely and nice. They are trusting and optimistic.

Brands which evoke this archetype:
McDonald's, Innocent Smoothies, Birdseye, Coca-Cola.

Brand motivation: Independence & Self-actualisation.

02. The Explorer

Wanting to break free from the norm, the explorer can never stand still. They value freedom and do not like being confined in any way. Always on the hunt for new experiences, the explorer sets off towards the horizon looking for adventure. For them it's more about the journey rather than simply the destination.

Brands which evoke this archetype:
Starbucks, The North Face, NASA, Land Rover.

Brand motivation: Independence & Self-actualisation.

---

31 In later years a more involved guide to archetypal branding has been released entitled "*Archetypes in Branding: A Toolkit for Creatives and Strategists*" by Margaret Hartwell and Joshua C. Chen (2012). This work treats each of the twelve archetypes as a main category and then splits each archetype into four sub archetypes giving the potential for a brand to embody one of forty eight sub-archetypes. If your team require further depth to their exercise the above book may be of help, however I have found that for most teams the twelve primary Jungian archetypes defined by Pearson and Mark are adequate.

03. The Sage

Sages are the gatekeepers of knowledge and truth. They seek out and use intelligence, data and analysis to understand the world. They like to backup their understanding with cold hard facts. They can be overly analytical and hate anything which misleads or that displays ignorance. They value wisdom and objectivity.

Brands which evoke this archetype:
Wikipedia, Google, The Economist, University of Cambridge, National Geographic.

Brand motivation:
Independence & Self-actualisation.

04. The Hero

Heroes are all about saving victims from some terrible enemy. Known for their courageous acts, they stand for proving their worth against the evil and rising to meet the challenge. They are most fulfilled when they overcome a challenge and fear becoming weak and vulnerable. Heroes value quality and efficiency and don't have time for things with no real substance or that do not help them triumph.

Brands which evoke this archetype:
Duracell, Nike, Fedex, British Army.

Brand motivation:
Mastery & Esteem.

05. The Rebel[32]

Seeking revenge or revolution, the Rebel is all about changing existing systems. They will disrupt, break or destroy in order to overturn what is not working. Their greatest fear is powerlessness or being viewed as inconsequential and so they strive to make an impact in everything they do. They are against the status-quo and are catalysts for change.

Brands which evoke this archetype:
Dr Martins, Apple, Harley Davison, American Apparel, Anonymous, Jack Daniels, Vans.

Brand motivation:
Mastery & Esteem.

06. The Magician

Magicians are about transformation. They are true visionaries and use win-win solutions in order to achieve success. They make change happen but there is an element of magic and mystery about how it will occur. Using their mystical ways the magician likes to make dreams come true. They are all about transformation and apply their skills to bring about change. Their passion is to find successful outcomes in everything they put their hand to.

Brands which evoke this archetype:
Polaroid, Mastercard, Disney, Lynx, Red Bull, Dyson, Cadbury.

Brand motivation:
Mastery & Esteem.

---

32 Mark and Pearson call this archetype "The Outlaw".

07. The Citizen[33]

Not wanting to stand out and perfectly content with being part of a crowd, the Citizen is all about belonging. All the Citizen wants to do is fit in. They seek to connect with others using empathy and are down-to-earth realists who love to celebrate the simple things in life. They are not ambitious or keen to rise above their station and hate to stand out. They fear being exiled and rejected and value being part of the group. They love practical solutions that benefit the majority.

Brands which evoke this archetype:
CitizenM Hotels, Ikea, eBay, Kit-Kat, Google, Capital One, Amazon, KFC, Volkswagen.

Brand motivation:
Belonging & Relationships.

08. The Lover

The Lover is all about sharing experiences. They focus on becoming as physically and emotionally attractive as possible and value deeply connected relationships. They are driven by passion for the ones they love and fear being alone or unwanted. This archetype does not only come in the form of sexual partnership but also of parental and family affection.

Brands which evoke this archetype:
Häagen-Dazs, Ann Summers, Channel, Gucci, Thorntons, Baileys, Magnum, NESCAFÉ.

Brand motivation:
Belonging & Relationships.

---

33 Mark and Pearson call this archetype *"The Regular Guy / Gal"*.

09. The Jester

Jesters exist to have fun and fill their lives with enjoyment. Living in the moment, having a great time and enjoying life is what they are known for. As captivating entertainers, they are often funny and playful. They use their talents to bring smiles to people's faces. They hate being bored and are always looking for things which are entertaining and enjoyable.

Brands which evoke this archetype:
Ben & Jerry's, M&M's, Fanta, MailChimp, Compare the Market.

Brand motivation:
Belonging & Relationships.

10 The Caregiver

Caregivers are selfless characters who exist to help others. They look after, and are protectors of, those weaker than themselves. They use what skills they have to look after and protect others from harm. They are all about hearty, cheerful service. They are often selfless and sacrifice their own wellbeing for others. They are people of compassion and generosity and struggle to get on with those who are selfish or not grateful for what they offer.

Brands which evoke this archetype:
Johnson's Baby, Nivea, Persil, NSPCA, NHS, Pampers, Boots, Bupa.

Brand motivation:
Safety & Stability.

11. The Creator

The character in the workshop, busily inventing new things which will make a huge impact to the story line. Hugely innovative. Full of ideas. Always thinking about new ways to solve problems. Creators are highly sought after for their conceptual thinking. They are always seeking to make something of lasting value - using their imagination to produce things. They desire to keep making and use skill and creativity to give form to their imagination. Their ideas can sometimes run wild and they can get frustrated when obstacles get in the way of what they are striving to produce.

Brands which evoke this archetype:
Lego, Canon, Adobe, Etsy, Pinterest, YouTube, Sony, Crayola.

Brand motivation:
Safety & Stability.

12. The Ruler

Wanting to lead their people to success, the Ruler (also known as the 'Sovereign') brings order and control out of chaos. They use rules & laws to great effect. They focus on creating a prosperous family or community. As strong leaders they take their responsibilities seriously. They fear anarchy and having their position overthrown.

Brands which evoke this archetype:
Metropolitan Police, Hugo Boss, IBM, Mercedes Benz.

Brand motivation:
Safety & Stability.

ACTIONS

The following series of activities are really fun and creative. Leaders often enjoy this section if it is presented in a passionate and articulate way.

There is a level of education involved before the group can enter into these activities. Be sure that whoever is leading the session is well versed in the principles outlined, as they will need to present and explain each archetype and will usually need to give examples of brands which are exhibiting each archetype's qualities. It is crucial the group grasps the reason why this step is helpful and why it is important they participate.

Ensure that the previous work completed on the 'Brand Triangle' and 'Audience Personas' are readily available for consideration as these will underpin the actions in this step.

Define your customer motivation & review your "why"

Purpose

Understanding your customer motivation can help to lead you towards an authentic archetype. Start with this.

Method

As a group, review your 'Key customer need' defined in step 2.

Consider which of the four 'customer motivations' your audience fits into. Are they trying to find safety, stability and control over chaos? Are they seeking to enhance the feeling of belonging and enjoyment? Are they needing to increase esteem and master risk? Are they looking for ultimate fulfilment and independence?

Next, review your 'Why statement' written in step 1.

Your customer motivation should be what is ultimately driving your brand - this basic motivation need to underpin your 'why' and authentically guide you forwards. Your brand should be *the* answer to their need. Your "why" needs to *harmonise* with their motivation. It may be that at this point you uncover a disconnect between your customer needs and why you believed your brand existed in step 1. If this occurs it might be worth reconsidering your 'Why statement'.

For example a healthcare brand with a customer motivation of 'Safety & Stability' might have a 'Why statement' along the lines of: "*We believe that the elderly should never be afraid of not having access to medical assistance when they need it*".

Define your archetypes

Purpose

Your archetypes will become the basis of your brand strategy. Selecting an archetype allows you to have a clear communications and behavioural framework.

Method

I would suggest beginning with some basic theory about how stories define meaning and how archetypes are universal characters found in stories across cultures and time. Explain to the leadership team that in this session they will be selecting a primary archetype.

Next, review each archetype. I typically suggest that the facilitator initially discourages discussion as each archetype is presented and then the team splits into groups. Each group must decide on a primary archetype and two secondary on their own. After a period of time, gather the groups together and, at this stage, open the session up for discussion around each group's decisions. Let the debate ensue!

If no clear agreement is reached, pause and consider the 'Why statement' and key customer motivations and use the brand archetype map to help.

These tools exist as guides only and there is no real right or wrong. The important thing is that the leadership team settle on one primary archetype.

If needed two secondary supporting archetypes could also be selected but I often find this leads to a diluted understanding of the brand personality.

Once selected it is worth testing the decision on a focus group of ideal customers to check if the archetype chosen resonates with them.

Brand as a person

Purpose

To help anthropomorphise the brand further and get the group to consider the brand as a person.

Method

Split the group up and get each subgroup to propose famous fictional or real characters which embody the value system, archetype and purpose of the brand.

Gather each subgroup around and ask them to list out their selections. Each group must justify why they have selected each character or person. These to be listed on a white board.

Once all the characters have been detailed, select two or three as a group which seem to embody the brand.

Note: if the groups struggle, it can be helpful to change tack and get the teams to nominate a colleague who embodies the brand instead of famous people or fictional characters.

Audience archetypes

Purpose

To add further meaning to your brand story by connecting each persona with an archetype.

Method

As a group, review each audience persona. Decide which archetype best fits each one. Ensure this is documented as you will use this later in the process.

You may find your audiences archetype is the same as your brand archetype and that's okay. It helps to clarify your relationship with your audiences. For example you will be a 'Hero' amongst an audience of 'Heroes'.

You may find that you are not the same at all. For example you discover you are a 'Magician' whose magic helps an audience of 'Citizens' to go about their everyday life.

Hopefully you will be able to identify your archetypes and begin to see how your brand fits into an exciting and compelling story.

OUTCOMES

Results

- **Customer motivation & review of your why statement** - a clear idea of what is motivating your customers and a considered, refined 'Why statement' has been clarified.

- **Brand archetype** - your primary archetypal character and personality type which you can use as the framework for adding meaning to your brand and telling your brand story, has now been agreed.

- **Brand personalities** - a review of the type of personality the brand will have has taken place. This will become the basis for how it might speak and behave.

- **Audience archetypes** - each persona will now have an archetype associated with them.

Through the process

Key strategic principles have been discovered, and defined by going through these activities. These decisions will become the basis of the brand story which we will now work on in the following sessions.

Your leadership team will have made some difficult choices as to what they stand for (and unwittingly what they do not stand for). If the process has been managed effectively they will also have become unified on these key, over arching principles.

04

DEFINE
THE EVIL

PRINCIPLES

It is impossible to stand for everything. You cannot be all things to all people.

In this step we will be considering what it is you believe. Knowing what you stand for is one thing. Knowing what you do not stand for is perhaps even more powerful. We'll also therefore be considering what you do not believe.

When you can communicate what you are and what you aren't, you will exclude your brand from some. But that's okay. You will attract more fervent and passionate followers. You will help your audience to identify with your brand because it will align with their personal belief systems. You will be better able to help your audience identify, because buying from you will say something about them.

It is also important that you keep tabs on your marketplace and review how your competitors are presenting themselves and behaving. This allows you to be distinctive, different and a clear alternative in your customer's mind.

You can't please everyone

It is very important that leadership teams lose sight of the idea that they are trying to sell products to anyone who will buy them. This is the factory approach based on the industrial era. As Seth Godin famously preaches; This mentality will lead to *"average products for average people"*[34]. The same principle applies to branding. As the saying goes: *"If you don't stand for something, you'll fall for anything"*. You will create an "average brand" for "average people". Your brand and its offer will end up looking like all the other offerings out there. There is no real focus, no real reason to buy, nothing to differentiate you from anyone else doing anything similar to you.

In my experience, this is the historical case with many business to business brands. But things have to change if you are to compete in today's global marketplace.

Shifting your mentality from selling anything to everyone to selling specific solutions to specific people, means that you will create better value and will be able to charge more for it. Stop just competing on price. Start competing on meaning.

Your focus will need to be on managing the meaning of your brand for a specific audience. You are seeking to create something which is passionately and loyally believed in by your audience and people. You are aiming to become the number one brand for that audience in that category and the employer of choice for your people. You want to be the brand that comes into their minds when they think about your relevant category. You want to be the answer to their very specific problems. This approach is more stable than trying to be all things for all people because your people and audience will fight for you and will not simply drop you when the next best thing comes along that's cheaper.

---

34 *'Surely not everyone'*, Seth Godin blog, June 3rd 2010, sethgodin. typepad.com/seths_blog/2010/06/surely-not-everyone.html

*"I have no idea how to
handle this issue"*

*"I have guiding principles to
help me to handle this issue"*

Having a brand manifesto which sets out your brand's
core beliefs, what it stands for and what it does not
stand for, is hugely beneficial. Unlike a set of "rules"
your manifesto becomes a statement of beliefs which
are a promise to yourselves of how you will behave as a
business and how you will communicate. It is essential
that you do not simply have a list of 'values' which
could become meaningless over time. I once worked
with a client who had a value entitled 'legacy'. After
countless interviews with staff members it became
apparent nobody really understood this. It turned out
that what was meant was that the brand was 'legacy
conscious' - keen to ensure the impact it made was
positive in the long term and not just the short. This
example shows the importance of being clear with
your meaning. I suggest that you always backup your
values with an example of how you expect that value
to be outworked in the experience of your audience.

For example:

We value TRUST.
Which means that we will always be
transparent and never lie or cheat.

This is a clear belief with clear guidance on
how it should be manifested by the brand.
This example is obviously quite generic. Try to
think of more specific values which affect your
audience and what they believe in and value.

Know your difference

Every good story needs some form of threat and tension. A Yin to a Yang. An evil Sauron whose hordes of orcs are a threat to the simple peaceful folk of Middle Earth in Lord of the Rings. A manipulative emperor who uses the dark side of the force for evil in Star Wars. A Professor James Moriarty to a Sherlock Holmes.

In these types of stories we are more ready to fall in love with the heroes because the evil is clearly defined. Put simply, we want the good guys to beat the bad guys.

You now know what you stand for and you have begun to define and better appreciate your audience. Together you are the "good guys". The next step is to consider the "bad guys" and to clarify why you are different.

By defining what you believe in, you, by implication are also declaring what you do not believe in. The stronger the definition of "evil", the more passionate your people and your audience will be able to get about what you believe in. The focus and vision of the "good" becomes clearer and the principles which govern your brand's behaviour are more natural. "*Of course we would not do that - it's against our principles*" your staff will be able to say.

In his book "The Culting Of Brands"[35], Douglas Atkin suggests that if you want a "cult-like" following and create a mutual sense of separation for your brand you need to:

1. Determine your potential franchise's sense of difference

2. Declare your own difference with doctrine and language

3. Demarcate yourself from the outside world

4. Demonise the other

---

35 *'You're different, we're different'*, pages 17-33, *'The Culting of Brands'*, Douglas Atkin.

These are all powerful principles which help you to clearly stand for something in the audience's mind. If a brand does the above effectively it can become a beacon to those who are discontented with the status quo. It will have a clear sense of differentiation.

In brand stories I believe there are various types of "evil" a brand is competing against:

- **Competition** - how others in the marketplace do business - for example your competition might tie customers into lengthy contracts.

- **Culture** - industry problems and injustices - for example traditional processes taking too long or not being in harmony with the environment.

- **Beliefs** - systems which affect behaviours - for example a belief in the need to reach a goal or in how people should be treated.

Brand Yin & Yang

Your brand's positives & negatives will attract people to your brand and repel people away from it.

What are they?

Know your competition

Reviewing the market place in which a brand operates is a very healthy thing to do - although be careful not to copy. The first step in reviewing competition is to ensure you know who (or even what) the competition for your product or service is. The best thing to do is to ask members of your target audience about this. Ask questions of your current customers like *"if we didn't exist, where would you go to solve XYZ problem?"* Searching online can also be helpful. Don't just search for what you do, search for the solution to your audience's problems. Competitors who were not on your radar before, might suddenly become the real competition you need to contend with.

When you have a list of competitors move on to reviewing how they are selling meaning to your audience. Do they focus on "what" not "why? How can you communicate a better and more emotional story than they are? Now we have the principles of brand archetypes in our mind's eye after the previous sessions, it is a good time to review our competitors in this regard. Are your competitors embodying an archetype? Is it the same as your chosen one? Get a spreadsheet together of all the competitors and map out their stories, vision and archetype.

Having done some research around this, it is also helpful to complete some classic 'Competition Analysis' to help you see your brand in the wider context of your category. This is not always possible, but when it is I have found it can lead to a few "eureka moments".

On the next few pages I have set out two basic tools which can be helpful. Ideally these would be completed with audience insights, maybe a customer focus group, as well as your leadership team.

Competitor Map

Mapping your brand competition can have huge benefits, as you can see the choice your audience has in one visual. This will also help identify opportunities for your brand. One of the best ways to do this is to consider a major need your audience has and then review all the brands which are seeking to fulfil that need. Consider the average price of products from that brand and the value they have in an audience's mind for fulfilling the need. Next, plot them on the below graph. If you can identify a "zone of un-met needs" you may have discovered an opportunity.

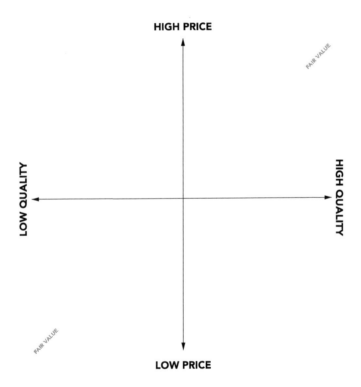

SWOT analysis

This model helps you get a better understanding of the strategic choices that you face. It is a helpful planning technique which can be used to identify the Strengths, Weaknesses, Opportunities, and Threats related to your brand's competition. Again, having these all plotted in one place can be highly productive as a leadership team can quickly see what they need to improve on and also what to focus on, to pursue their brand's vision.

	HELPFUL	HARMFUL
INTERNAL	**S** Strengths	**W** Weaknesses
EXTERNAL	**O** Opportunities	**T** Threats

ACTIONS

By now the process should be gaining momentum. Up until now we have been quite positive. We have looked at what the brand stands for, what it believes and why it matters. We've considered who the brand serves and we have started to consider how the brand might begin to behave and communicate.

Now we will sharpen up on the brand's vision and think in positive and negative ways about its belief system.

We will also review the competition and consider where the brand sits in the consumer's mind. We can review how different our current communications really are in the marketplace and what we might need to do to tell our story in a clearer way.

Brand manifesto

Purpose

To review and clarify what the brand stands for and what it does not. To define the brand's sense of difference.

Method

Review the brand's "Why" and "How" statements set out in step 1 and in particular the values (key beliefs or behaviours) which were previously defined. If you feel that the original statements need amending to bring them more into focus, now would be a good time to do this. Write out the brand's "statement of beliefs" in a clear way. Start with a word which encapsulates a value and then give some examples of how you would expect that value to translate to your audience. *"This means that..."*

Consider the selected brand archetype and the values that are being set and see if there is anything within the archetype which needs to be outlined in the values.

Also consider the work that has been done in relation to the competition and what they are claiming. If they are defining what they stand for and it is similar to what you would state, you may need to go in stronger.

Once this has been done, review each value and write the opposite of the positive statements. What do you not believe in or stand for? How would you expect this *not* to translate to your audience? *"This means we will never..."*

Define your competition

Purpose

To have a clear idea of the marketplace the brand is operating in.

Method

As a group, go back over your audience personas and write out their 'needs'. Next, work out and agree the key information you will be using to compare your brand with the competition. For example: 'name', 'website URL', 'social media links', 'archetype', 'vision', 'values', 'price point', etc. Create a comparison table for each group to fill in. Split the leadership team into groups. Each group is to take a need (or a couple of needs depending on what needs have been identified and the size of your team) and systematically review the competition for the specific audience need and fill out the table. If you do not know the competition for that need, some research into your audience would be highly valuable to help inform this process. For this reason it is useful to have members of your audience with you in this session because it is all about perception in the audience's mind - not yours.

Once you have a series of needs and competition filled out in your table, move on to plotting them on a 'Competition Map' (or better still, get an audience focus group to plot them). It is helpful to have your brand plotted on these competitor maps too. It can enable you to see where the brand is now, but also where it might need to move to.

Once this is done, fill out a SWOT analysis. This will help you define your findings in one clear table.

Regroup, then have one person from each group review each need and give an overview of where your brand sits in relation to the competition.

OUTCOMES

Results

- **Competition review** - research into your audience's needs has been accumulated into a SWOT analysis and Competition Map.

- **Brand manifesto** - a statement of beliefs in both the positive and negative has been defined.

Through the process

Your leadership team will have been empathetic with your target audience enabling future decisions to be based on their perspective.

The brand will have been considered in the context of the wider marketplace.

You will have considered what you do not stand for, as well as what you do. This will further help define the meaning of your brand.

05

PUT YOUR BRAND STORY TOGETHER

PRINCIPLES

All the elements are now in place to define your brand story.

Similar to typical stories, brand stories need to be engaging and contain all the elements of a traditional narrative.

We now have the key archetypal characters and the elements required to build a basic plot. This stage of the Storyategy process is all about how you put them together in a way which is clear and easy to communicate.

Taking principles from archetypal plots, we will piece our story together in a compelling, emotional and exciting way.

Every story needs a simple plot-line

Why do we tell stories? We tell them to make sense of things, to share wisdom, to give ourselves a sense of belonging.

The great thing about a story, is that people instinctively connect with it if they can relate to the characters or the situation described. Through the characters and the plot, it can help them make sense of their situation. It helps to explain who they are and what they believe. It sets a comforting, emotional pathway into the future which can then be practically executed.

For this reason, stories are memorable, create a deep emotional meaning in our minds and cause us to take action. They are the key to branding - the management of meaning. Stories are everything.

At its top level, every story tends to follow a similar pattern and it's no different with brand stories.

The simplest I've come across[36] is as follows:

- **Beginning** - setting of the scene and introduction of the characters.

- **Middle** - tension is introduced, a conflict arises and there is a significant problem with the world in which the characters exist. This disturbs the dreams or progress of the main character.

- **End** - the solution to the problem and the satisfactory ending of a changed world, which no longer contains the tension. They all live happily ever after.

This is the basic structure of a typical, recognisable story.

---

36 This was actually first promoted by the ancient Greek philosopher Aristotle (384 BC - 322 BC) in what is known as the 'Dramatic structure.' After explaining the 'beginning', 'middle' and 'end' of stories he also states: "Well constructed plots must not therefore begin and end at random, but must embody the formulae we have stated." Aristotle, Poetics, 1450b, c.335 BC.

There are only seven basic plot lines

In the monumental book "*The Seven Basic Plots*" by Christopher Booker, he explains that, just as there are archetypal characters in stories, there are also archetypal plot lines (or 'meta-plots').

In his book, Booker reviews these plot lines in depth, showing how they appear across cultures and time and are simply recycled with new characters. Storytelling has been around for thousands of years, so it is unsurprising that we, in effect, tell the same stories over and over again as we seek to make sense of the world around us. It is part of our human condition.

At some point in the lives of your customers, they will experience, in some small way, one of these seven archetypal plot lines. Which plot line is being played out right now in your customer's lives? Where is your brand in the story? Unlocking this will allow you to tell your brand story effectively.

Here is my summary of the basic plots based on Booker's work[37]:

Overcoming the Monster

The main character is forced to overcome and destroy an evil monster (this could also be a system, person or circumstance) which threatens them or their world. After the monster is removed order is restored. Not only this but the main character has become well respected.

Examples of stories which use this plot line: The War of the Worlds, Star Wars: A New Hope, Beowulf, Dracula, Day of the Triffids, Jaws, Nicholas Nickleby, Pocahontas, Jack and the Beanstalk, King Kong, Avatar and the James Bond franchise.

Helpful for brands: seeking to assist their customers in gaining a victory.

---

37 For deeper insight into these I recommend that you read '*The Seven Basic Plots*' by Christopher Booker, Bloomsbury, 2004.

Rags to Riches

The main character begins the story in a wretched and destitute state, severely lacking in some aspect of their lives. As the story goes on, they have some initial successes, gaining and acquiring things which improves their situation. At some point however, they face crisis and lose everything they have gained so far. They then pull themselves back up and recover everything they lost. In this process they grow as a person and can focus on what is important in life (usually not the riches).

Examples of stories which use this plot line: Harry Potter, Cinderella, Pinocchio, Jane Eyre, A Little Princess, Great Expectations, Oliver Twist, Aladdin, David Copperfield, Game of Thrones, The Prince and the Pauper, Charlie and the Chocolate Factory.

Helpful for brands: who help customers show their natural talents to the world so they can improve and enrich their lives.

The Quest

'Quest' plot-lines are focused on a search for a special item, place, or person that requires the main character to leave home in order to find it. Along the way many frustrations, obstacles and temptations are presented, before one final test is overcome against all the odds and the quest is completed and the item, place or person is found.

Examples of stories which use this plot line: Treasure Island, Around the World in 80 Days , The Pilgrim's Progress, The Lord of the Rings, the Indiana Jones franchise, The Voyage of the Dawn Treader, Ice Age.

Helpful for brands: who assist customers in a long term goal, departing wisdom, guidance and support to them along the way.

Voyage & Return

This plot involves the main character going to a strange and mystical land. Some evil enters this land which has to be overcome. Once this is done by the main character and the threat is removed, they return home having learned a valuable lesson.

Examples of stories which use this plot line: Alice in Wonderland, Goldilocks and the Three Bears, Peter Rabbit, The Hobbit, Gone with the Wind, Cast Away, Chronicles of Narnia, Apollo 13, Finding Nemo, Gulliver's Travels, The Wizard of Oz.

Helpful for brands: seeking to assist their customers in reaching or coping with an unfamiliar place.

Comedy

Comedies do not follow a rigid structure and most romances fall into this category. These plot lines follow a pattern where the main character has to untangle an adverse circumstance resulting in a happy ending. Typically, along the way there is light hearted and cheerful humour brought about by the characters or circumstances which surround the plot, although it is important to recognise that 'comedies' do not need to be 'funny'.

Examples of stories which use this plot-line: Groundhog Day, Mr. Bean, Honey I Shrunk The Kids, The Mask, A Midsummer Night's Dream, Zoolander, Hancock's Half Hour.

Helpful for brands: who look to add value through entertaining customers.

Tragedy

Tragedies tell of extremely difficult times and end in a bad way. The main character has to face horrible circumstances, usually has a huge flaw or makes a terrible mistake which becomes their downfall. Often this flaw is not recognised by the main character until it is too late and there is no going back. Typically, the foolishness of their mistake serves to teach a valuable lesson.

Examples of stories which use this plot line: Romeo and Juliet, Of Mice and Men, Titanic, Macbeth, Julius Caesar, Breaking Bad, Hamlet.

Helpful for brands: who seek to sympathise with customers who are in difficult situations.

Rebirth

Rebirth plots are where the central character usually goes downhill morally. Due to a series of important events in the story they change their ways to redeem themselves. At the end, the previously morally bankrupt character has been revitalised and reborn into a noble or better person.

Examples of stories which use this plot line: A Christmas Carol, The Frog Prince, Beauty and the Beast, The Snow Queen, The Secret Garden, Despicable Me, Megamind.

Helpful for brands: who want to effect positive change in their customers.

Sometimes it's helpful to have some examples. Here are two I have come across:

The example of Rebel Kitchen

On their website[38] food product Rebel Kitchen state:

> "Rebel Kitchen was born out of a need to redefine health. It's time to change our approach – from what constitutes health, to how we make food and how businesses operate within the food space.
>
> It's a different kind of health message – one that doesn't separate the individual from the whole, and one that is based on actions instead of preaching – because it's all connected."

Here we can see that they start their brand story with why they exist. The purpose behind their existence is to "redefine health". They define the "evil" subtly - ethically questionable food producers.

This is none other than a typical "Overcoming the Monster" plot line. The brand is clearly the "Rebel" (clue in the name!) archetype looking to disrupt and rebel against the norm. This emotional story will resonate with their audience - the ethically conscious person looking to be healthy. This promise can never be broken.

The example of Nando's

Eating at a Nando's is a unique experience. The staff, the smells, the decor and of course the food. The success of Nando's is born about from a very clear and focused brand experience which means that it can be consistently applied. On their website[39] they outline their brand story as follows:

> "PERi-PERi is the heart and soul of Nando's. Its story is our story. For centuries the people of

---

38 www.rebel-kitchen.com/about-us/ May 2018
39 www.nandos.co.uk/our-brand-story/ May 2018

*Southeast Africa have used PERi-PERi to bring
fire to their food. It is in Mozambique's rich soil
and blistering sunshine that the African Bird's Eye
Chilli grows into its fiery best. When Portuguese
explorers arrived there, they were enchanted by
its flavour. They added a squeeze of lemon and
a kick of garlic and turned PERi-PERi into a very
well-travelled spice. Which is how, many years
later it ended up in Rosettenville, Johannesburg.*

*One afternoon in 1987, two friends went for lunch
at a humble Portuguese eatery. As their meal drew
to a close, they knew they'd tasted something that
had to be shared. PERi-PERi was about to make one
more journey – from Rosettenville to the world."*

This story follows the "Voyage and Return"
plot line. The two friends in a mystical land,
who discover the secret of PERi-PERi - only to
return with it to share their experience.

The brand therefore embodies the "explorer" archetype
helping customers escape the norm and discover
new exotic flavours whenever they experience the
Nando's brand. This promise must never be broken.

Brand stories have to be authentic

Brands cannot afford to tell lies or dress themselves
up to be something they are not. Gone are the days
when a slick advertising agency could fool a consumer.
Today, customers can communicate with each other by
leaving reviews and even starting anti-brand campaigns.

The more "virtual" and online our lives get, the more
consumers want brands to be genuine and consistent.
The brands they choose to join need to not only 'walk
the walk' but also 'talk the talk'. They want every
aspect of their experience with a brand to live up
to its promise, its 'why' and its belief system. They
want consistency with the emotional story it tells.

From viewing a website, to using an app, to walking around a store, to speaking to customer service, to unpacking a product - if the customer experience does not measure up to the brand promise, in every aspect, customers become increasingly disenfranchised.

On top of the marketing communications, the way brands behave is a huge influencer on the level of loyalty shown by customers to that brand. With customers having access to a vast amount of information and news, if a brand behaves inconsistently with its values, it will be discovered and customers will act. The truth will out and untold damage will be done.

One has only to think of the recent customer boycotting of big brands, such as the coffee shop Starbucks for allegedly avoiding paying tax on their British sales back in 2013. In relation to this the Huffington Post ran an article which stated *"Starbucks reported its first ever fall in UK sales last year, during a period when it was hit by a customer boycott over its tax payments"*[40] . Although the company used legal mechanisms in its tax affairs, it provoked public outrage when it was discovered it paid hardly any UK corporation tax. This appeared to go against its brand promise *"To inspire and nurture the human spirit – one person, one cup and one neighbourhood at a time."*[41]

This led to some customers arranging boycotts and protests at the chain's cafés. Yes, this customer led protest (known as 'tax shaming') was undertaken on moral grounds but it was also fuelled by the fact that Starbucks' brand promise and values are in contrast to its reported tax affairs. This led to Starbucks backtracking and offering to voluntarily pay twenty million pounds in extra tax.[42] This example is one of many we could site but it goes to show the power is in the hands of the consumer not the seller.

---

40 'Starbucks Suffers First Ever UK Sales Fall In 2013 After Tax Boycott' Huffington Post, 25/04/2014.
41 "Our Mission" as stated at time of print, April 2018, Starbucks, www.starbucks. co.uk/about-us/company-information/mission-statement.
42 'Starbucks bows to outrage and offers £20m extra tax', The Telegraph, Matthew Sparks, 6th December 2012.

Gaining insight into customer attitudes by keeping on top of focus groups, social media comments and customer surveys are great ways to ensure that a brand is delivering on its promise. If it's not, customers will soon let you know. They aren't afraid to air their grievances. If something in their experience of your brand doesn't measure up as being 'genuine' it will get called out.

It is therefore essential for the modern business to innovate, continually review themselves in the light of their brand story and their customers' experiences and continue to seek to close any gaps.

Mantra for within. Motto for without.

Do brands need a mantra or a motto? Some people make this an either or type of question. My view is that both are powerful tools as you seek to manage the meaning people attach to a brand.

Both a "mantra" and a "motto" are a short, pithy phrase about the brand. They should be no more than five words long. They represent a set of beliefs, ideals or an ethical stance that the brand takes. They both will explain "why" but from different perspectives.

Here is my definition of the meaning of the two ideas:

- **Mantra** - represents the brand to the staff and suppliers of the brand.

- **Motto** - represents the brand to the outside world - to prospects and customers.

In other words, a mantra is for "within" and a motto is for "without". These sayings, once defined, can become very powerful tools in a business. Two sides to the same whole.

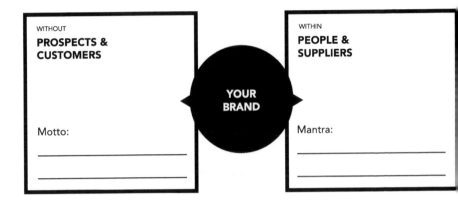

A brand mantra

A mantra should define everything a brand is and will be one short, snappy and memorable line. It should do this from the perspective of the staff of the company.

It helps all employees and suppliers understand what they need to focus on, in order to deliver the brand experience effectively to the brand's audience. They help to filter out nonessential behaviours and keep everyone on track.

It should encapsulate 3 key things:

- **An emotion** - this will be born out of the 'why' of the brand story.

- **A description** - this will loosely define 'who' the brand serves.

- **A function** - the 'what' of the brand boiled down into one word.

Typically a mantra would not explain what the brand

does in terms of product, sector or service. Your mantra and motto are bigger than that. This is not detail. This is the stuff of brand dreams and aspirations.

It is also important to point out that a brand mantra is not something you would typically use publicly. Your mantra should be a rallying cry to others who believe what you believe - to attract great people. The mantra should be a concept blanket which covers everything. It should be the guiding principle by which your people operate.

A brand motto

"Think different" (Apple), "The king of beers" (Budwiser), "Finger Lickin' Good" (KFC), "Because I'm worth it" (Lorel), "Make believe" (Sony), "The Ultimate Driving Machine" (BMW).

These mottos represent brands to their audience. They encapsulate the meaning of the brand to the consumer. The power of them is obvious. They summarise in an easily memorable way the emotional meaning of the brand, drawing and attracting customers to their rallying cry.

Their value is in connecting external communications together. A consistent promise which is uttered over and over in TV adverts, websites, social media and in any other communication there is from the brand to its audience. These little sayings get into the heads of customers and stay there. They help people remember you.

Mottos should again only be 2-5 words long. They should ALWAYS communicate 'why' the brand exists. On top of that, the following themes are prevalent in the most successful brand mottos:

- Memorable

- Emotional and resonate with the goal, challenge or dream of your audience

- A message which suits the brand story and archetype

Once a business has a motto which summarises its 'why', they attach it to every communication they can. It is placed under the logo and it is shouted from the rooftops. This is done to make sure the brand lives it.

Again I feel it's helpful to have a few examples here:

The example of Nike

The famous sports brand, Nike, is a good example of a brand which utilises a motto and a mantra.

The mantra: "*Authentic Athletic Performance*". Emotionally "authentic", it serves "athletes" with the function of better "performance". This mantra guides and focuses its people.

The motto: "*Just Do It*". This evokes the 'hero' archetype, rallying its audience to join the brand cause. The phrase resonates with people who are looking to succeed in fitness and sports. It speaks to their hearts. It is the essence of why the brand exists - to help people achieve success.

The example of McDonald's

The fast-food chain McDonald's plays on its 'innocent' archetype really effectively.

The mantra: "*Fun Family Food*". This is how it represents the brand internally. Emotionally "fun", it serves "families" with the function of "food".

The motto: "*I'm lovin' it.*" This encapsulates what the 'fun family food' should mean to its customers. The convenience of fast-food and love of spending time with the family is what this brand 'means'. It's why it exists to customers from an emotional point of view.

The brain & storytelling

If we go into the science[43] of what happens with the brain when a story is told, we find different hormones being released which cause emotion.

Most stories begin with the problem or the danger. When danger hits, we get a dose of cortisol, the fight or flight hormone. It helps us pay attention. As the story continues and we learn things, we get dopamine which makes us feel good after learning. Finally, when the threat of danger is removed and the problem is resolved we get a dose of oxytocin, 'the love molecule'.

These chemicals are drugs. Basically, stories make us feel great. This is why we, as a society, are hooked on stories - from Hollywood blockbusters, to the telling of our nightmare journey to work. They give us meaning. They evoke our emotions. We love it. We are addicted.

It is worth considering how customer centric a brand story is. Make your story not about you, but about your customer's problem being removed and give them a hit of oxytocin. It is this we are all craving and by telling your story right, you can evoke this deep emotional connection with your audience.

---

43 For example see Forbes, '*This Is Your Brain On Storytelling*', July 21, 2017, Giovanni Rodriguez www. forbes.com/sites/giovannirodriguez/2017/07/21/this-is-your-brain-on-storytelling-the-chemistry-of-modern-communication/#6611298ac865. See also the Youtube video: '*Future of StoryTelling: Paul Zak*'

ACTIONS

During this stage, a full review of all past activities and their end results is helpful. These ingredients are going to help produce a delicious story.

We are now going to boil it all down into a simple but powerful emotional narrative, which will sum up exactly why the brand exists and why.

It will be summed up in such a way, that it will immediately engage the right audience on an emotional level.

It will speak primarily to their hearts and then to their heads. It will become the basis of all future activities for the brand and be able to inform business and marketing strategy. It will especially be helpful as a foundation for how the brand presents itself visually.

Your one page brand story

Purpose

To create an authentic brand narrative for your brand. The 'elevator pitch' that excites, engages and resonates with your target audience.

Method

Review the simple "beginning, middle, end" plot sketch which was completed in step 1[44]. The chances are this will need to be completely re-written in the light of what we have reviewed over the following sessions.

Remind the group of the brand archetype, the 'why' of the brand, the cause it stands for and the evil it is seeking to eradicate.

Review your core brand audience personas and their archetypes.

Next review the 'seven basic plot lines'[45] and, as a group, discuss which plot line might best fit what your audience is looking for from the brand. Send each member of the group away to write a one page document along the lines of the plot line selected.

The story must:

- Include your industry context.

- Be customer centric (including detail on their goals, challenges or beliefs).

- Be archetypal in nature both in the characters and the plot line.

---

44 See page 25
45 See pages 85-89

- Be deep-rooted in the brand purpose, why it exists and what it stands for.

- Explain what the brand does not stand for and the 'evil' it resists.

- It must be authentic.

Gather the group back together and get each person to read out their brand story. As a group, discuss and vote for the best one. Perhaps discuss how it could be edited to further include some of the other ideas presented if this is needed but be careful not to dilute or complicate things. Less is more.

Once you have a one page brand story, get this typed up. This will be the "long version" of the story.

The final task will be for the group to make a "short" story. This must be no more than two paragraphs. Work out what the essential elements of the story are. Focus in on the "why" of the brand.

Put these to one side. When the brand's 'tone of voice' is completed (this happens in the final Storyategy step) it is a good idea for a professional copywriter to review these 'long' and 'short' stories to ensure they are articulated in the brand's tone of voice.

You may also want to consider having a few different versions compiled with slightly different emphasises and tone. Put these through some audience testing. The results could be insightful and allow you to make any necessary adjustments to ensure the meaning obtained is exactly what you desire.

Your mantra & motto

Purpose

To produce a very memorable mantra and motto which can become the core of everything the brand stands for.

Method

Review the brand story, archetypes and values. The leadership team should go away as individuals and, using no more than five words, attempt to summarise the brand story for those within. What should the brand mean to our people? Gather the leadership team together and see what everyone has got for these mantras. Debate and refine accordingly.

Now review the customer needs and customer archetypes. Remind yourselves of the archetype you are embodying. Now go away as individuals and write your brand motto. What does the brand mean to customers?

In each case, your five words should communicate why the brand exists and what it stands for. It should encapsulate the brand narrative in the long and short stories.

Again, it might be worth adopting audience testing to validate your decisions.

OUTCOMES

Results

- **One page brand story** - a refined brand story will now have been written based on the seven basic plot lines and the work completed thus far. This will be in a 'long' and 'short' form.

- **Mantra & Motto** - two summary statements for communicating what the brand stands for to audiences without and to people within have now been documented.

Through the process

The leadership team will have further focused what the brand stands for, making important decisions on how to articulate the meaning they want their audience and their people to attach to it.

The simplicity of the brand mantra and motto means that the real essence of the brand will now have been uncovered and defined.

Well played.

Now you have defined your brand story. It's in your leadership's hearts and minds.

But now you need to tell it. You need to live it. You need to get the same story within the hearts and minds of your audience.

It's essential you do not stop now...

06

SET A
STRATEGY
FOR LIVING
YOUR STORY

PRINCIPLES

This step, is all about how you will tell and live your story in a consistent way.

- It's all well and good having done the exercises thus far with your leadership team; however the principles defined and the valuable work completed, now need to be cascaded down through your organisation in order for it to influence culture.

You need to set your business up for success.

To do this you need to put your discoveries down on paper, so that if people move on, the ideas and brand principles will not.

You also need to bring accountability to the brand.

In this final section of the process, I've outlined ways in which this can begin to be done.

This step will be very specific to your business and context. Therefore, I'm sure there will be many other ideas you might wish to use. Get creative!

A brand strategy needs to be written down

I would suggest that the brand strategy
is one of the most important documents
your business could produce.

A brand strategy is not a business or marketing strategy.
A business strategy is a high level plan for reaching
specific business goals. These are typically growth goals.
A marketing strategy is usually a response to a business
strategy, in how marketing will be used to reach
those goals. These strategies are typically set out or
reaffirmed on a year by year basis with details of regular
activities, marketing channels, metrics and budgets.
Business and marketing strategies are temporary.

A brand strategy is altogether different. It is eternal
and universal. It should outline the sum of all of the
items we have looked at in the process thus far. It
should define the brand, why it exists, the audiences
it is serving and the narrative which needs to be told
to those audiences. It outlines how the brand should
communicate. It is the high level principles upon which
the brand operates. It should underpin the business
and marketing strategies that the company produces.

A brand strategy is the emotional compass of the business. It should be inspirational. In my view, an effective brand strategy should be punchy, engaging and clear. Ideally it should be no longer than 20 pages long, with each page containing no more than 400 words. When writing up a brand strategy, I typically ensure it contains the following areas:

- **Brand triangle** - defining the 'why', 'who', 'how' and 'what' of the brand.

- **Brand audience** - personas the brand exists to serve.

- **Brand personality** - the brand archetype.

- **Brand manifesto** - what we do and do not believe in.

- **Brand story** - one page emotional brand story which describes why we exist, with a compelling beginning, middle and end.

- **Brand mantra & motto** - 3-5 words for 'within' and for 'without'.

The benefits of having an effective brand strategy documented and in place are:

- **Unity** - your people can unite around a clear vision of what the brand stands for, enabling joined up and effective decision making. You have a foundation on which to continue to build your brand.

- **Clarity** - you can communicate clearly, allowing for prospects and customers to understand exactly what you deliver and why. You will get more consistency in your collective behaviours and communications.

- **Connectivity** - it becomes easier to attract and begin dialogue with new prospects because they quickly understand what you stand for. You acquire loyal customers quickly because your prospects' experience with you supports everything you say.

On the flip side, if you do not have a brand strategy in place, then the negatives are:

- **Anarchy** - your colleagues and communications will pull in different directions because nobody appreciates what the brand stands for.

- **Confusion** - you will have no clear plan to continue to build your brand. Prospects will be confused as to what you deliver. It will be hard to attract customers because they won't understand what you stand for. It will become increasingly difficult to retain customers because their experience with you is inconsistent.

After you have gone through the previous Storyategy stages it is well worth putting together a brand strategy document and circulating it with all of the key stakeholders in the process. This ensures that everyone can be on the same page. If there are any final minor conflicts, resolve them now, because typically the workshop style process of discovery would end here and the real work begins of living your brand.

Once a brand strategy is in place, your marketing team has a framework to look at how they can take that story and tell it effectively. If you have physical spaces, such as a retail store, the interior designers have a basis for decision making - indeed, because it is a clear, emotional strategy, it can become the basis for any creative brief. I've known these used in HR and induction packs to help with hiring and set expectations of new employees. I've also seen these used as a check point for business decisions.

As time goes on, the universal principles it contains can be referred to again and again. If you want to create a business that is customer centric with a consistent story, then your brand strategy will become the guide to all decisions which affect customers.

Create a 'visual language' which tells your story

First impressions are really important. If you meet someone and something does not 'feel' right about them, it takes a lot for you to warm to them again. The same is with branding. How a brand dresses is the basis of how it communicates. How it conveys meaning is just as important as what it says or claims - especially at the initial stages of a relationship with a potential customer. Once you have your brand strategy in place, work with a creative design team on how the brand should dress.

Brand identity

One of the key elements of how a brand dresses, is the consistent marker or symbol which it marches behind. Typically this is called a 'logo' a left over term from the ancient days of printing where specialist blocks were created by printers. These were termed "logo-types" or "logo-marks" and were a single piece of type, from which was printed a word, a group of separate letters, or a mark. I prefer the term 'brand identity' - the key graphical identifier of the brand.

Whilst important, I believe way too much attention is given to these single little graphical monsters.

Having worked in design agencies for the last 16 years, it amazes me how hung up business leaders can get over their logo. It's like they want to cram everything they can into their tiny little graphic, as if this is how meaning is going to be conveyed to their audience. Design iterations go back and forth, back and forth, back and forth. Hours of time are wasted on 'logo design' which will have little or no impact on the bottom line - if anything, a hugely complicated end design could have a negative impact.

Think about all of your audience touch points that the modern brand communicates through:

websites, email, apps, print, signage, advertsing and at point of sale in retail environments. How does it do this? Through a myriad of techniques: speech, written word in fonts, images, video, audio. It does, in effect, communicate like a person.

The meaning that a customer attaches to that brand will not be only derived from the logo but from all these other aspects of how and what is being presented around the logo. Meaning will be derived ultimately from 'what' and 'why' it is that the brand exists. Therefore a brand identity 'system' is required for the modern brand - not simply a 'logo'. I call this a 'brand visual language'. The logo will barely be seen in isolation. Meaning will be communicated via this wider visual system.

The pinnacle of this system should be the mark or symbol the company holds up as its emblem - but this is not there to communicate every little thing about the business. It is there so that the customer can recognise the brand. For this reason it is essential the brand identity is kept simple.

A logo is simply a label. A sign post.

Like a person's 'name' the brand identity is used to differentiate the brand swiftly. It is there to help customers recognise that what they are looking at is from that organisation.

Elaborate illustrations, vast arrays of colour - I've seen them all. They only 'sign post' a viewer to a competitor because people want simplicity not complexity.

Simplicity also says "confidence". It says clarity. It says "I know what I'm about". This is the type of meaning consumers desire.

Some of the most successful brands simply have their name written out in a basic font[46]. Do not fall into the trap of trying to tell your audience all

---

46 For example: Calvin Klein, Sony, Google, Disney, FedEx, Skype, Vimeo, Lego, Cadbury.

about yourself in your brand identity graphic. Keep it clean and remember it is simply an identifying mark. It's a label or sign post. Nothing more.

If you do decide to redesign your brand identity, it is worth considering that with a shift in dominance from print to screen, brand identities can afford to be more flexible in their use of devices and elements. In today's digital world, brand identities can be more dynamic[47]. Don't be too rigid with exactly how the brand identity is to be displayed. The key point is that it is recognisable every time it is seen. Modern brands should also consider how their identities will animate and display in videos[48].

Modern brands often need to represent themselves in the small, confined space of an icon. For example on social media. Therefore if your brand identity was created before social media, the chances are that it's time to review it in the light of the new era we are operating in.

Without getting hung up on the detail, it is important that the brand identity is in keeping with the brand archetype and story of the brand.

The example of Fanshawe College

Fanshawe College in Canada have an interesting brand identity[49], which I like to champion whenever I can because of its story telling quality. Their logo mark is unique. It has four "Fs" which have been arranged to look like a star which they call 'NorthStar'. According to the college this has been designed in this way for the following reason:

"NorthStar is the symbol of Fanshawe's pathfinding commitment. Because of its essential role in navigation

---

47 For examples of 'dynamic' brands consider: M-TV, City of Melbourne, OCAD University and the Design Academy Eindhoven.

48 With the rise of voice interaction technology, another aspect of brand identity is how the 'logo' sounds. If the brand were to appear in audio only how would it present itself?

49 Designed in 2014 by Trajectory, trajectoryco.com.

over millennia and across many different cultures, the north star is known by many descriptors: Polaris, pole star, lode star, guiding star. Polaris stands almost motionless in the sky, and all the stars of the northern sky appear to rotate around it. That makes an excellent fixed point from which to navigate. Fanshawe's NorthStar is made up of four letter Fs that come together to represent all points of the compass to create multiple pathways to explore. It's a powerful metaphor for our role in helping people find their way, whatever their goals. "[50]

The "explorer" archetype and the story the college tells of helping guide students to their destination in life, is therefore embodied in the brand identity of the college. This is a stunning example of a brand identity which is a symbol of why a brand exists but also a good example of a very simple label or sign post in terms of execution.

---

[50] Fanshawe College Brand Guidelines v4, April 2017. See www.fanshawec.ca/about-fanshawe/corporate-information/brand-toolkit for more information

Brand visual language

Most of the time your logo will be seen by your audience in context. For example on your website, on a brochure, on social media, on your building signage, etc. In all of these instances the context will be more important to the viewer than the actual logo. The meaning that a viewer will attach to your brand will be based on the surrounding messages and communications. The logo is just a label for these, so the consumer attaches them to your brand.

Therefore how you surround your logo with messages, images and communications is more important than the logo itself. What are you saying? How are you saying it? What will this mean to the viewer? These are the real "branding" questions overlooked because we are obsessed with "logos".

To communicate effectively and consistently across multiple marketing channels, all of the methods for communicating need to be considered in line with the brand story. Consistency is the number one rule. The colours, fonts and images the brand will use to differentiate and communicate with its audience and the layout systems that it uses will need to be considered and defined.

Like choosing your clothes, these things need to be carefully explored because the impression you give will add a huge amount of meaning in the eyes of the beholder. In today's digital world you sometimes only have a few seconds to connect emotionally with your audience. If it doesn't "feel" right, they will swipe on to the next brand which does connect with them. Nothing personal - it's just modern life.

As an example of this, imagine you were looking for some accounting software for your business. You need a flexible solution which is reliable and trustworthy. You came across a Google ad for a cloud based software package claiming to offer what you need and solve your problems. You hit the advert - only to find yourself presented with highly entertaining cartoons of a jovial nature presenting the product to you. Would this 'Jester' style visual language "feel" right for your serious business need? No, it would jar and you would move on - not because the software did not do what you needed it to do but because it did not "feel" right. The brand story was not being told in a way which evoked the 'Sage' (for knowledge) or 'Sovereign' (for control) archetypes you needed it to. The story was not being told well.

How do we help audiences feel 'right'? Partly by what we say, partly by how we say it. Well thought through visual design is the key. Design which looks unique and attractive to the needs of our audience, communicates effectively. Design which underpins the brand story we are telling, solves problems of ambiguity.

If you are printing packaging or producing printed materials, consider the paper stock and weight you are using. Does this help to tell your brand story or hinder it? Does it help add the right meaning to your communications? The right experience to the customer journey?

Having a strong visual language ensures that whenever your brand communicates, it is clear to the consumer that the communication is from your brand. You need to be doing something in a unique way - preferably that nobody else can do.

One test which can tell if you have a strong brand language, is to cover up your logo - if the marketing communication can be recognised as coming from your brand then you know you have a strong identity.

I like to challenge creative teams I am leading, to produce a visual language which tells the brand story in one style of image. This forces creative teams to strip back the complexities of a brand story and focus on the core. For example if the brand archetype was a 'magician' then how could we tell the story of transformation in one image? If we are telling a 'sovereign' story how can we show control out of chaos?

The answer to these types of questions will be unique to the business category, audience and brand story you are seeking to portray. These answers though, are crucial to developing a visual language which is effective, unique and meaningful.

Having a concept by which in one image these archetypes can be evoked, and yet subject matter and details can be changed, is preferable so that the narrative can continue to be told into the future.

But my number one tip would be: keep things simple.

The example of Nando's.

Nando's is a brand we have mentioned before[51] because of its explorer brand story. However we will refer to it again because it also stands out as an amazing example of a brand with a well thought through, meaningful, visual langue based on their brand story[52]. The brand uses a distinctive quirky headline font. Why? They claim they were inspired by traditional South African sign writing. *"So, we asked Marks Salimu – a South African sign-writer and talented artist to help us out. Marks hand-painted all our letters and characters onto wooden panels and these were made into our new, refined font."*

As the meaning of the brand originates from the food produced in South Africa, this is a master stroke. It communicates authentic meaning to its audience. It tells its "explorer" based story - evoking a sense of a new experience. Suddenly when you are reading words from Nando's you are now reading from a more 'authentic' typeface.

51 See page 90.
52 The Nando's visual language was designed by South African consultancy
   Sunshinegun in 2016. See also: www.nandos.co.uk/our-brand-story/

What about its secondary font? *"In search of a secondary font for when we have to write longer things than headlines, we looked to Johannesburg, South Africa (the vibrant city where Nando's was born) for inspiration and found the answer in the road, adopting the same font that's used on road signs throughout South Africa. The font used is straightforward, legible and because it pays homage to our roots, it's perfect for helping you navigate your way around Nando's."*

Nando's uses patterns in its brand language. Why? *"Silhouettes and patterns are big in African design. So when we created our new look, we chose to have a local NGO design and create three beautiful patterns especially for us. To honour our roots, they have African, Portuguese and Nando's touches in just the right places."*

What about the colours of the brand? *"We're so passionate about PERi-PERi, we wanted to make it our official colour. So, with a bucket of African Bird's Eye Chillies in hand, we asked Manie Pietersen – a specialist colourist with 24 years' experience in mixing and matching colours – to help us decide the exact colour of PERi-PERi. He nailed it and we've called this colour PERi-Red! It's not the only colour you'll see at Nando's. Black plays a big role, edgy neons add pops of colour and secondary colours – which we've drawn from our restaurants and Southern Africa – complete the mix."*

This 'visual language' communicates the meaning of the brand. It enhances the brand story. It underpins it. This can only be done when a brand knows its soul, the story it wants to portray, why it exists and why its audience should care. The reason why this is so powerful for Nando's is that this creative thinking would be so hard for a competitor to mimic. It is unique to them because only they (at least on a global scale) are offering a dining experience of this nature stemming from this part of the world.

Usage guidelines

Once you have worked with a design team to establish the way your brand will dress and communicate creatively, be sure to document your findings. In times past usage guides were defined in PDF documents and assets were placed in file systems which could be accessible and distributed easily. The problem with this is that if, over time, additional guidelines were added or new templates updated and produced, it became hard to manage all of the versions of styles which appear. Now, modern businesses are creating these guides online, as it means they can update them, and wherever any one of their teams or suppliers is in the world they can access the latest assets[53].

However you decide to communicate and maintain your brand's visual system, the principles you set will become the guide to future design and marketing teams, to enable them to communicate consistently. To help get buy-in, it should not just be a list of do's and don'ts but should also communicate why the brand is presenting itself in a certain way.

I would suggest you need to review every customer touch point in the light of these usage guidelines. Ensure you are communicating visually in a consistent manner across them all - from your website and the user experience it encourages, to the interiors of your offices and retail stores. Everything must be consistently delivering on the narrative of your brand story, otherwise doubts of authenticity will creep into the mind of your audience.

53 Writer and brand strategist, Jess Thoms details some brilliant examples of online design systems in a blog post she has written for InVision: 'Your guide to design systems from the world's leading brands', October 9th 2017, www.invisionapp.com/blog/design-systems/ .

Document your tone of voice

Another area which would be well worth exploring is the type of words your brand will use. I would suggest working with a team of copy writing experts to help enhance your brand personality. Share with them the work you have done on the brand archetype and the brand as a person. This will enable them to create principles of how the brand should speak to its audiences. They will set an overall tone of voice and consider how this will work at the different stages of the customer journey.

Again, document how the brand will speak and write in a set of tone of voice guidelines. Present these to your staff to ensure how they speak and write, reflects the personality of the brand's character.

Set out how your brand will behave

For your brand to truly succeed, the brand strategy will need to be communicated to all levels of your organisation. It particularly needs to be understood and embodied by the people who are speaking and dealing with customers.

In his book "Brand New"[54], Wally Olins explains:

> "The people who work in a big organisation have a multiplicity of cultural, socioeconomic, religious and natural affections. If they are going to develop a genuine corporate loyalty, what they do, how they do it , why they do it, how it contributes to the strength of the whole has to be clearly set out and interpreted for them in a way they can understand, grasp and commit to. As part of all this they have to absorb what is and what isn't acceptable behaviour"

---

54 'Brand New', Wally Olins, Whames & Hudson, 2014, page 70.

This is one of the hardest things to do in a large organisation, where the leaders are far removed from those on the 'coal face'. A culture around your brand story needs to be cultivated and developed. But what's the best way to do this? Here are some ideas:

1. Brand launch

Once you have the brand strategy documented and your brand usage and tone of voice guides in place, it would be a great time to launch your brand to your team. The "brand launch" would be held off-site. Your CEO or Managing Director could introduce the journey you have gone on, explain the brand story and define the meaning behind the brand. Nothing beats a passionate and rousing rallying cry. From this you could have other speakers who then communicate the values of the brand and how they will be celebrated, as well as the new brand identity, visual language and tone of voice for the company. This might also be a great occasion to invite clients and stakeholders or perhaps even do a private brand launch just for them.

2. Personal development

After the brand launch, I would suggest that every opportunity to communicate and remind your teams of what the brand stands for should be taken, especially in relation to personal development within the company.

Your values should become part of the personal development reviews and plans held with staff. For example, at a regular appraisal ask brand related questions such as:

- Do you believe you are contributing to why our brand exists? If so how?

- How are you helping to fulfil our brand vision?

- Describe how you feel you are you living out each of the brand values in your current role?

- What habits have you introduced to help you remember to live our brand values?

These could be graded[55] and tracked, or at least commented on to encourage personal commitment to the brand story and values.

In his book "Traction", Gino Whitman suggests a scheme in which a reward (such as a gift voucher) is given out on a week by week basis by a team member who awards a colleague for exhibiting a company value. The person doing the awarding has to email every member of the company and explain the story behind why they believe their colleague exhibited the brand value. Next week it is the turn of the person who won the award to give it to one of their colleagues. This way the company values are seen to be celebrated and a culture of exhibiting them can be fostered.

3. Hiring

A famous (and some say mythical[56]) advert allegedly posted by Antarctic explorer, Sir Ernest Shackleton in the London Times Newspaper stated:

> *"Men wanted for hazardous journey. Low wages, bitter cold, long hours of complete darkness. Safe return doubtful. Honour and recognition in event of success"*

When hiring, the most successful people will be the people that believe your brand 'why'. These will be people who already hold the brand's values as their own personal values and belief systems. These people will be the best fit to help reinforce and maintain your desired brand culture.

---

55 For example out of 10 or via marking each as: unsatisfactory, satisfactory or exceptional.
56 See Campaigns "History of advertising: No 137: Sir Ernest Shackleton's 'men wanted' ad", June 18th 2015, www.campaignlive.co.uk/article/history-advertising-no-137-sir-ernest-shackletons-men-wanted-ad/1351657#PVgz6Rt5LU3lRgYb.99.

Like Shackleton's advert, it is essential you seek out people who believe the same as your brand. Shackleton was not simply looking for sailors. He was looking for people who desired exploration and adventure. His advert was not about what a candidate could do but why they did what they did.

He could have written something like:

> "Candidates wanted for a long seafaring journey. Ten years' experience minimal. You must be able to navigate by the stars and read a map."

However the advert is not about 'what' but 'why'.

As the story goes, Shackleton's expedition went badly wrong. It ended up with his crew being stranded for almost two months on the ice. Amazingly they all came back alive because morale and discipline were maintained. Team work and collaboration meant they looked after one another. This was not by chance. Shackleton had surrounded himself with people who shared his 'why' and believed what he believed.

When hiring, it goes to show that it is important you hire for mind set. Don't just look at what skills the candidate offers. Look at what they believe and why they do what they do. Skills can always be taught.

I would also highly recommend that when a new colleague is on boarding, the brand story is communicated to them. Their induction process into the company should explain to them "why" the brand exists and the "values" which they are expected to adopt and embody. The brand 'mantra' needs to be hammered home. It is essential they understand the guiding principles of the brand story in order to live them.

4. Internal visual prompts and communication

The brand story, or elements of it (e.g. the brand vision, mission, values and mantra), should be hung up in prominent staff only zones. These could be printed on walls in staff rooms, displayed in toilets or be printed onto posters to be displayed around warehouses. Have your mantra printed up on the wall in your board room. Visual prompts help to ensure your people do not forget the governing principles of the brand and what is expected of them.

Internal communications should also embody the visual language and tone of voice. Leaders should seek to reinforce the brand principles whenever the opportunity arises.

Live your brand

Commitment to the brand is crucial. The leadership team which has created a strong brand culture, needs to ensure that they are committed to embedding this in the organisation. A method of accountability should be created by the leaders, so that they themselves can ensure they are living the brand values and embodying its archetype. Perhaps consider how you will remind yourselves of the brand and its story at your regular leadership meetings. Maybe you could grade how you all feel the company is living up to its vision and values every year. Have someone collate how the company scored out of ten and review your findings at your quarterly reviews. This will keep the guiding principles of the brand strategy within the consciousness of the leadership team on an ongoing basis and also help to consider areas for improvements.

Of course building and maintaining a strong brand will also mean that you are producing products, services and experiences which deliver on the brand story. Your brand has to be authentic and all the work done up to this point will be undone if your brand behaves in a way which damages its reputation, or goes against what the brand stands for.

For this reason, the brand strategy should be considered when developing new product ranges. Do these new products fit with the brand strategy? Ensure your brand behaviour matches your values, archetype and brand story.

Likewise your marketing strategy needs to closely align with the brand strategy. How you choose to communicate and present the brand to new audiences in order to grow is important and needs to be in keeping with the brand strategy.

There are many ways you can ensure your brand story is going to be lived. I don't have all the answers to how this might best be done for you and your organisation, however I'm sure you will think of your own ways to do this.

Here are some initial ideas which might help:

1. Track sales and marketing based on personas

Some of the work we have done on brand personas can become the basis of your marketing strategy. The approach of tailoring customer experience around personas is a whole line of discipline but one which can help you reap huge rewards.

For some businesses, a digital 'inbound' marketing strategy would fit well with the persona work we have completed. Conversions on the website can be segmented in a Customer Relationship System and as prospects go through the sales process, they can be taken through a customised journey to help increase sales close rates. Your sales funnel can be strategically considered, tracked and tailored to better succeed. Forecasting can become easier.

2. Align your brand with similar archetypal influencers

The work completed on which archetype the

brand is, can highly inform your marketing efforts if you were thinking of using influencer marketing. Identifying popular people who embody your archetype and approaching them to endorse your products on social media or host your events, will enhance the brand story in your audience's mind.

3. Brand membership club

You need to develop your audience from simply being consumers to being members of the brand. The work completed in 'designing' your ideal customer can become the basis of creating a 'members' club - for people who believe what you believe. Through this the values of your brand can be celebrated. Think about holding an awards evening. Through events, you can help build your brand community and further help your audience towards success - all the while reinforcing your brand story and enhancing your brand's reputation. You will genuinely be standing up for your purpose. Find ways to create status and exclusivity.

4. Allow your audience to tell your story

The brand story is powerful but it is still what you are saying as a business. Authentic stories by your audience are more powerful because they reflect an authenticity about the meaning your brand has had in the real world. It is well worth considering what channels you have open to listen to your audience and enable them to tell their own stories of how the brand has impacted their lives. Consider creating regular ways of collecting stories from your customers - perhaps through a section on your website or via competitions on social media. These stories can be used to reinforce your communications.

Remember that your marketing tactics will change over time but your brand principles should be eternal. Do not be afraid to change how you are communicating and building your brand's audience.

ACTIONS

We are now at the final stage of the Storyategy process. These last exercises have been designed to help you set your business up for success. Really, they are more about documenting, planning and implementation than creating anything new at this point.

You might be tempted not to put these into practice but you must else your hard work is liable to be forgotten over time.

To help you tell and live your brand story effectively, to ensure you are living your brand, these foundations need to be in place. Resist the urge not to do them and ensure they have priority on your action points.

Take the project over the finish line.

Then the job of living the brand can really begin.

Brand strategy

Purpose

To ensure you have a written, well designed and engaging brand strategy which everyone in the business can be proud of and get behind.

Method

Review the section above on 'Brand Strategy'. Consider, from the leadership team, who best can articulate this and get a well written and designed document together. If you have in house design teams make steps to pull together a project team to work on producing the document. If you do not have internal creative resources, allocate a budget and engage with a creative agency who understand what you are trying to achieve.

At this stage the brand document does not have to be elaborately designed, nor does it have to completely reflect your current brand style if you hope to review your brand identity and visual language. It does however, need to be well written and cover all the key points listed on page 108, as well as anything else your leadership team feel is essential to the brand.

Once you have your brand strategy document in place and the leadership team is happy, you can then move on to implementing it.

Consider setting up independent research to regularly report on how your audience are perceiving your brand against key criteria. Keep checking in on how your strategy is working and track any progress.

Foundation design principles and documents

Purpose
To ensure the brand has a consistent
way of dressing and speaking.

Method
Review the pages about the brand's 'visual
language' and 'tone of voice'[57]. Allocate someone
from the leadership team to oversee these aspects
of the project. Typically, a marketing manager
would be the one to pick up this responsibility.

If you had in house creative teams you could engage
them, or you could go externally to a creative agency.
The aim will be to come up with the visual style and
tone of voice and then document this into usage
guides. These guidelines should explain the visual
system, which will underpin how the brand presents
itself to the outside world. User testing and research will
be essential to ensure what is produced is effective.

The way these creative teams work will be different
from team to team. Select which approach suits your
time lines and budgets. Above all, ensure that the team
you engage 'gets' the principles of brand storytelling
and understands the archetypal approach. The last
thing you need, is for all your hard work to be undone
in the execution of the look and feel of the new brand.

Create and distribute documents, or better yet,
produce a website for these core elements, so that your
people can easily access and use them. Remember,
everything produced must have at its core, the brand
story defined in the brand strategy. After you have
completed these, it might be worth updating the design
style and wording of the brand story completed in step
5[58] to ensure that it is in line with the new brand style.

---

57 See page 110-116
58 See page 99

People management systems

Purpose

To encourage and ensure the brand
is lived through your people.

Method

Allocate someone in the leadership team to have
responsibility for cascading the brand story down
through all levels of the organisation. Review and
implement a plan, which should be regularly reported
on. It might contain things on the following subjects:

Leadership - set up a system so the leaders
are reviewing the brand, it's values and how
it is being perceived on a regular basis.

Recruiting - review job adverts and check that what the
brand stands for and its values, are part of the recruitment
process. Review how interviewees are assessed and ensure
elements of the brand's values are included in the process.
This will ensure new staff believe what you believe.

Induction - review how new staff are onboarded
into the company. Produce an induction pack
which introduces new team members to the brand
culture and spells out what the brand stands for.

Training and reviews - consider how existing
staff can be consistently trained in the brand's
ethos. Consider how personal reviews between
managers and staff can be used to communicate
and celebrate, the brand values and expectations.

Rewards - consider implementing a reward scheme
for staff who embody the brand values.

Communications - internal communications should
regularly go out to staff members. Come up
with ideas as to how your brand story and values
can be amplified in these communications.

Touch point audit

Purpose

To ensure you are presenting your brand consistently and your customer experience is 'on brand'.

Method

Appoint a leader to be in charge of rolling out the new brand story across every aspect of the customer experience. You could consider engaging an external agency to help with this roll out, or having a dedicated team pulled in to focus on this.

Go through every touch point along your customer journey and review what the persona is thinking, feeling, doing and seeing. This should be considered from all your audience's personas.

Make a note of areas which need to be improved, and set up a plan to ensure the brand story will be consistently told throughout. Your website and digital footprint will need to form part of this review.

Consider ways you could encourage your audience to tell stories and share them.

For internal audiences, review how you are reinforcing the brand's values and story. Identify initial areas where you can effectively position the brand mantra, motto and values so that they can be seen. Wherever you can, you need to help your people live your brand, so ensure that staff only areas (like canteens, staff rooms and the like) contain some form of branded elements to remind staff of the brand and company expectations. Consider hiring an interior design business to assist in ensuring the brand story is communicated in physical spaces.

Get a plan together for implementing.

Launch event

Purpose

To celebrate the work done so far and to unveil the brand to your people in a positive way.

Method

Once you have the basics of the way the brand will present itself in place, it is time to begin communicating this through your organisation. Appoint an organiser (either someone in your team or an outside event organiser) to set up a company wide event, or series of events, to launch the brand.

As an employee, it is exciting to know that your leadership team are forward thinking and that the business is getting to grips with what it stands for. Launch events can also be done for suppliers and even dedicated customers.

Ensure that the brand story is articulated in a positive way to every member of staff. Perhaps consider producing a booklet and giveaways to make the event memorable. It might be worth having a few speakers from the leadership team allocated to present, excite and inspire your people. I always find the best launch events are ones which articulate the journey that the leadership team has been on, then when the final brand story and visual language is unveiled, the audience can understand why it is the way it is. Don't forget the practical impact the new brand style will have on staff and ensure you address the key ways that the brand will be presenting itself, how staff will be trained on the new assets, the basics of the tone of voice and any other areas where staff might need support.

The key thing is to excite your people. To reinforce what it is you stand for and the greater picture they are all contributing towards.

OUTCOMES

Results

- **Brand strategy** - a document defining all of the work completed thus far will be available.

- **Usage guidelines** - 'visual language' and 'tone of voice' will now be in place.

- **People Management Systems** - plans for implementing and maintaining the brand principles within your leadership, staff and brand audiences will have been made.

- **Touch point audit and implementation plan** - a plan which ensures the way the brand communicates will roll out effectively.

- **Launch event** - a plan for launching the brand and communicating it effectively to your people will be in place.

Through the process

The leadership team will have considered and given responsibility to specific people to lead each area of the brand roll out.

What the brand stands and its meaning for will be articulated.

There will now be systems in place that ensure the brand is continually lived and not forgotten in the years to come.

Nice one.

Well done you. You've got to the end. I'm sure the process has been challenging but the decisions made along the way will, I hope, be highly valuable to you as you seek to build a brand which has real meaning.

I wish you all the very best. Keep on keeping on, until your brand vision comes to pass.

OUT

TRO

IT'S BEEN A PLEASURE

You've got this

I hope you have found this book helpful and the ideas and tools I've shared have been of interest. They are by no means the only way of enhancing a brand and as time goes on no doubt new methods and techniques may add value to the principles I've set out in this book.

One thing I am certain of though, is the universal human attraction to story telling will not change. At the end of the day we, as humans, will always be seeking to add meaning to our lives through stories. Good brands are ultimately good stories.

Strategy and story will continue to be a potent mix for businesses seeking to make an impact.

So as you engage with the discipline of adding meaning to what you do, I wish you all the very best.

May you tell your story well.

Special thanks

I thank God for all of His blessings.

A special thanks goes to my wife and family for their continued support, love and patience in putting up with me writing this.

Thanks to Christina Avraam for proof-reading and sense-checking the first edition.

I would also like to thank the hundreds of people who have commissioned me to conduct their brand strategies and workshops over the last 17 years. Without you this book would not have been written and the ideas contained herein would not have been sought out, defined or explored.

I have attempted to give credit to everyone who has influenced me in forming the Storyategy process throughout this book. I could not have written this book without the huge influence of the following writers who deserve a special mention: Simon Sinek, Margaret Mark, Carol S Pearson, Douglas Atkin, Marty Neumier, George Booker and Gino Whitman.

About Matt Davies

Matt is a creative brand strategist with over 17 years professional experience. He is a passionate advocate of using storytelling and 'archetypal' branding as the basis for marketing and business strategy. His work has helped businesses of all shapes and sizes discover and communicate their purpose and meaning. Brands he has worked with include Boots, Specsavers, Experian and Willmott Dixon as well as many other small to medium-sized businesses.

Matt began his career in graphic design but he's always been obsessed with strategy, purpose, creative concepts, human motivation and the principles of producing magnetic brands.

Over the last 10 years Matt has personally been involved in leading and delivering hundreds of projects on behalf of clients and has a wealth of experience in working with leadership teams to overcome challenges. His communication skills and ability to think creatively, empathetically, strategically and technically, set him apart.

After freelancing and working for agencies in London and Nottingham in the early part of his career, he founded and ran a branding design agency (Attitude Design) in 2008 which he led for nearly 9 years. At the end of 2016 he sold this to a larger digital marketing agency. Since then he has held various creative leadership and consultancy positions including leading the creative design team at Capital One UK.

If you would like to connect with Matt, he'd love to hear from you.
Email: mrmattdavies@me.com   **Twitter:** @mrmattdavies

NEED HELP?

You are not alone.

Matt is availible to consult and lead workshops.

Check **mrmattdavies.me** for his availiblity and also to read up on his latest thinking on his blog.

15066948R00082

Printed in Germany
by Amazon Distribution
GmbH, Leipzig